Advance Praise for *Never Part of the Plan*:

"Mike Shaw's inspiring journey from the bottom of the deepest valley to the top of highest peak is as powerful as it is uplifting. A tale of strength, courage, and perseverance, the former professional skier turned incomplete quadriplegic, turned motivational speaker's positive outlook on overcoming challenges will leave you feeling as grateful for having learned from it as he is for having lived through it. So, whether you're searching for a light at the end of the tunnel, or simply looking for a thought-provoking story to submerge yourself in, Never Part of the Plan is a must read."

—JEFF SCHMUCK, *Editor*
Forecast Ski Magazine

"Inspiring! Written from the heart. An authentic and vulnerable sharing of Mike's tragic accident, and how he was able to rise above the challenges, learning and experiencing the power of gratitude. A practical life handbook to motivate and empower every one of us."

—TREVOR JÄHNIG, CFO & VP of Finance
Tolko Industries, Ltd.

"Mike is a hero to all who meet him, and hear his story. Working hard to achieve purpose and success in life is the 'stuff of heroes,' and, when you add obstacles he has and is overcoming from his accident, you have a powerful example of how a guy from Vernon can become a hero."

—DR. DOUG NELSON, Ph.D.,
Nelson Education Consulting Group, Ltd.

"Mike's ability to overcome adversity is unparalleled. After going through any athlete's worst nightmare, he's taken a seemingly tragic experience and used it to motivate, inspire and uplift everyone around him. Many of the tools and outlooks he uses in this book, I was taught firsthand by Mike, and went on to win an Olympic Gold Medal. Even if you're not trying to win the Olympics or overcome a life altering injury, there's something in this book for everyone!"

—CASSIE SHARPE
2018 Olympic Champion

"Loved this book! Such a heart-wrenching story, it was hard to put down. I really appreciated the focus on mindset and gratitude the book took in the second half, as well. It was entertaining, and has a great message! I'd recommend it to all readers."

—DAVE WEALE, Entrepreneur & Coach

"A truly inspiring story of turning a life-changing accident into a positive situation through perseverance!"

—KEVIN HILL
Two-time Olympian & X-Games medalist

"Mike tells us of his own terrifying and terrific story while offering firsthand and practical insights into the world of personal development. This book is the quintessential hero's tale with Mike explaining his own emotional journey. Identity, self-doubt, mindset, values, goal setting. I loved how he touches on so many key elements that can not only take a person from the dark places in life, but can help you reach the pinnacle of performance."

—TOM SWIECICKI, Head Coach & Event Coordinator
Silver Star Freestyle

NEVER
PART OF THE PLAN

A STORY OF COURAGE RESILIENCE GRATITUDE

NEVER
PART OF THE PLAN

A STORY OF COURAGE RESILIENCE GRATITUDE

MIKE SHAW

Mikeshawski Media
British Columbia, Canada

ISBN: 978-1-64826-640-9

Printed in the United States of America

DEDICATION

To all readers—this story is for you.

CHAPTER 1

CHANGES

"I can't move! I can't roll over!" A tortured pause. "Colin!" My voice broke as I began to realize my worst fear.

"Just breathe, Mike! Keep breathing—I've got you!" Colin Sutherland instantly crouched over my limp body, assuming the position he needed to hold for the next forty-five minutes—on his knees and elbows, holding my helmet, keeping my head still in C-Spine. He should have put on his gloves beforehand, but there was no time—yet, frigid temperatures didn't deter him from holding me perfectly still. "Call ski patrol! Someone call the medics! We need the medics!"

Within minutes, a young ski patrolman arrived, quickly assessing the situation, then engaged his radio. "Dispatch—I need support! I need all hands on deck, I need the team, and the on-hill doctor! I have a code black!"

In that moment, I knew it wasn't good.

Then, I heard him again. "Code black! I repeat, code black! Get here NOW!"

Although Colin was in front of me holding my neck as I lay face-down in the snow, I could barely speak loudly enough for him to hear. "My neck . . . there's a sharp pain in my neck."

"Okay—hang in there." A few seconds later, the words I needed to hear. "They're here, Buddy. They're here . . ." Colin tried not to move me as he shifted his weight slightly. "You'll be okay!"

But, I knew.

Thoughts I didn't want to entertain flooded my mind as I lay almost lifeless. "Colin . . . I'm scared." Even though I thought I was yelling at the top of my lungs, my words were muffled as I struggled for each breath directed downward into the snow.

"Just breathe, Mike. Keep breathing. I've got you . . ."

Honestly, it hadn't occurred to me I might stop breathing. But, in those moments of fight or flight, my lungs were working overtime at half of their regular capacity—my diaphragm was partially paralyzed.

Then? My mind went into overdrive. *What happened? How did I get here?* As Colin held my head, I knew it was over.

I'd never ski again.

In that moment, my life gained a certainty I never considered—I'd probably ruin my parents' retirement, and I'd have to depend on them for the rest of my life. "What happened? I should have landed that trick!" I wanted redemption!

But, it was something I knew I'd probably never get—and, I still didn't understand what happened. I was performing a routine trick demonstration for my athletes and, as I flew gracefully through the air, I finished rotating out of a 720, two full rotations, taking off, and landing forward. "I swear I was going to land on my feet! What happened?"

"You did, man—you did! But, you landed and pitched forward onto your head!"

Then, I remembered! I landed on my feet, only I couldn't feel it! My nerves were cut off so fast it didn't register. Landing in soft snow caused me to pitch violently forward onto my head and neck, my feet shooting overhead like a scorpion's tail. With the devastating force of the impact, the entire weight of my body went straight to my neck, bending my head so far backward, something had to give.

It buckled.

My neck dislocated and snapped so fast, it opened in the front like a Pez dispensing candy gizmo. My spinal cord was crushed, and I didn't realize I landed feet first—all I felt was the massive uppercut as my face hit the ground. It was like no other crash—I couldn't stop falling. I couldn't bounce back.

I couldn't self-erect, getting back to my feet.

Then, nothing.

Lying motionless in the snow until my team arrived at my side felt like an eternity and, in those moments, I was certain—life, as I knew it, was done.

I was paralyzed. A quadriplegic.

Barely alive.

Chapter 2

THE BACKSTORY

December 16, 2013, started out like every other day, really—except I was on a ski trip with my team, accompanied by ten athletes, an assistant coach, and three parent chaperones. High in the Rockies in Summit County, Colorado, we were training vigorously for two weeks while some of the team were competing in the first World Cup half-pipe contest of the winter.

As you can imagine, morning air in the mountains is frigid—the kind of crisp forcing me to wake up even if I weren't ready. The instant I opened the door that morning to head to the car so it could warm up, cold air perked up my senses as I made my way down the front stone steps, snow shimmering in the morning sun.

I was in God's country.

Tuning into the day's beauty—sun, zero clouds—it felt like a perfect day for half-pipe skiing, and I was pretty sure my team would feel the same way.

Speaking of my team, it included several of Canada's top half-pipe talent ready to compete at one of the biggest contests of the year—the U.S. Grand Prix of Freeskiing half-pipe event at Copper Mountain outside of Denver. Although it was early in the winter, it was one of the most important contests my athletes would ski during that season.

A big deal.

At age twenty-six, I had the good fortune to coach very talented young athletes, my team a compilation of topnotch talent from each Canadian province producing half-pipe skiers. Not only was it a great privilege, it was a dream come true to work with skiers at that level. And, because my athletes skied on the World Cup circuit, it meant I was on the World Cup circuit—I got to ski the best, worldwide, half-pipe venues with my athletes during training days. I didn't have to demonstrate the same tricks, but I could if I were feeling up to it.

Once I started the SUV, I headed back to the house filled with enthusiasm to make sure everyone had their butts in gear—after all, it was the last training day before the big event. Four of my athletes were competing in the U.S. Grand Prix at Copper Mountain and, on that training day, we only had three hours to train in the pipe—from nine to noon.

Like any coach, my athletes were important to me—the reason I committed so much of myself to my team. Coaching is a selfless role, endlessly giving to the team, often going above the call of duty.

It was a labor of love.

My athletes' success was my success, so, for Brendan, Cassie, Lukas, and Garett, I was all in. That day would be the best day of skiing we had in the season with perfect conditions—it couldn't have been better! It was fitting, too—my four athletes deservingly qualified for the World Cup.

Brendan was the team's rookie—oozing with talent and a care-free approach to skiing the half-pipe, he was climbing the ranks quickly. Although quiet, compared to what one might expect from a high-flying skiing daredevil, what he lacked in words, he made up for in action. A cerebral and methodical skier, when the time came, he let his skiing do the talking for him.

He qualified for the U.S. Grand Prix above some of the more veteran skiers. With a compact frame and broad bone structure to support an ideal athletic physique, he was a coach's dream when it comes to identifying talent. While I expected him to have as many apprehensions as anyone in such a significant event, he was living up to his carefree, easy-going nature. With no expectations to perform at his highest level—at *the* highest level—so early in his skiing career?

For Brendan, it was all fun and games.

Cassie—the only girl on my team for years. She learned to keep up with the boys and, as time passed, she out-skied the majority of men I had the pleasure to coach. Cassie grew up on Vancouver Island with parents passionate about the skiing world. Her dad was a manager at the local ski hill, Mt. Washington, where Cass learned to ski, and she chased her brothers around the mountain, following them off the biggest jumps they could find.

A force to be reckoned with in the half-pipe, she would later become an Olympic Champion as well as one of the most decorated female half-pipe skiers of all time. But, during that day's competition training at Copper, it was all about preparing for her personal best. Her goal was to lay down the run for which she trained while using the event as a launchpad to move on to our Canadian National Team, as well as the Olympic Team.

The other two guys? They deserved to be at the U.S. Grand Prix as much as anyone. Garett was a veteran on the team with a work ethic and an array of skills making him a strong competitor. In that event, Garett had the ability to showcase those skills, proving he belonged on the world stage as one of the best. His contest preparation was all about performance and the pressure was on, wanting to do well—and, there was no question in my mind he would succeed if he followed through with his training.

Luke was also poised to make waves in the half-pipe skiing world. Tall and thin with wiry strength, he oozed talent and a carefree attitude, embodying the 'free' in freestyle. Like a cat, he could land on his feet from almost any twist, flip, or spin, making it look effortless. Not overbearing, when he showed up to ski, he always flipped a switch allowing him to assault the half-pipe with his trick mastery.

He was also the glue keeping the team strong—everyone liked him. He wasn't one for many words, but always one to contribute to the conversation with a bulletproof, dry sense of humor. He, too, was stepping up his game to compete in the Grand Prix—after all, it qualified as a World Cup competition. That year, Copper would be Luke's first World Cup start—even so, he was only granted a starting spot in the competition because a national team athlete was injured, pulling out of the contest. Technically, Luke was the wild card in the event, getting the last-chance opportunity to compete.

So, once everybody was ready to go, we loaded into the SUV and headed to the ski hill, playing our favorite songs of the day to help get in the zone. Although it wasn't competition day, the team had a lot of work to do in the pipe to refine tricks, as well as dial in their contest-ready runs. Sometimes, it's a mental game as much as physical in half-pipe skiing.

Half-pipe skiing and snowboarding are characterized as high-risk, high-reward acrobatics and, when athletes descend the twenty-three-foot tall, seventy-foot wide, six hundred foot long man-made marvel of modern engineering, a lot of risk is involved. Even though the site is among the best in the world and prepped to perfection with safety in mind, there is minimal margin of error for the skiers.

Made of concrete-like, hard-packed snow, big crashes were something to avoid—even so, athletes were required to perform five or six high-flying tricks to put together a competition run. Sometimes, competitors would flip twice, spinning up to three-and-a half times in one rotation, linking tricks together, forward and backward.

I'm not going to lie—it's scary.

With anticipation and electrifying energy in the SUV, we pulled into the parking lot, looking up at the magnificent contest venue. A few minutes later?

We were off to the lift, skis over our shoulders, feeling as if we could conquer the world!

Once we got to the top of the half-pipe, my skiers' goals were simple—dial in their contest runs. For Brendan and Cassie, it didn't seem difficult—they were feeling confident and well prepared based on our prior few days in the pipe. Luke and Garett had a bit more work to do, requiring them to perform more tricks that day than the others. "Ski with purpose," I urged, not wanting to waste valuable time. By doing so, they'd knock off tricks on their to-do lists to get ready for the contest which was only two days away.

Training commenced and, when the pipe opened, it was like a gun blasting at the horse races. Nearly sixty of the world's best half-pipe skiers began their performances, assaulting the pipe with skiing tricks and mastery. Multiple skiers sliding back and forth, taking air in excess of fifteen feet above the edge of the half-pipe peak, narrowly avoided each other as they descended. But, what's cool is it happened naturally and without collision—so much so, it could have been choreographed. After the first few runs, skiers spread out so they could get to work trying their highest degree-of-difficulty tricks, putting together contest runs without risking collision.

It's kind of weird—time fades when achieving the focused state my athletes were in that day. Brendan, Cassie, Luke, and Garett skied their hearts out, completing the three-hour training session with fear, commitment, frustration, and elation. Over in what seemed like an instant, Brendan and Cassie finished training feeling on top of their game. Totally stoked, they were smiling because both completed their five or six contest-ready tricks, and felt ready to compete—which was important.

But, by the time it was done, the emotional rollercoaster took its toll on Lukas and Garett.

The end of the training session marked the last opportunity my athletes would get to practice in the half-pipe before the event. It was a doubleheader with snowboarding, as well, so the snowboarders got the pipe for the rest of the day—their contest was the next day, and ours was the following morning.

On the day of competition, we would only get forty-five minutes to warm up in the pipe, which translates to two, maybe three, practice runs. The chair lift takes about fifteen minutes at Copper Mountain, so the amount of practice was limited. What that meant for my athletes was on their third or fourth run of the day, they would have to do their hardest tricks all at once with the judges watching. The pressure was on.

Brendan and Cass were handling the pressure, and they felt good and ready to ski in the contest, so their plan was to go home to rest up before the event.

Lukas and Garett were smiling, too, but more nervous, feeling the butterflies. It wasn't for a lack of trying, but they didn't get all of their tricks done. Their frustration was building, and pre-competition anxiety set in. But, as practiced by the U.S. Navy SEALS, "You don't rise to the occasion—you sink to the level of your training."

True.

Peak performance falls back on preparation, so it was understandable the boys were anxious.

Being a passionate skier, competitor, and coach, I knew they needed to take their minds off of the event for a bit, taking it back to the purity of the sport.

They needed to have fun!

So, we planned to set off to Keystone's Area-51 terrain park to hit a few jumps. I made a deal with the guys they could practice their half-pipe tricks on the jumps and kickers, then take those tricks to the pipe in just a day-and-a-half.

We left Copper Mountain and headed to Keystone, a short drive. On the way, we dropped off Brendan and Cassie at the team house, then picked up two more bodies—my friend, Colin Sutherland, and one other athlete, Ty Schulte. Ty was eager to ski, but Colin was nursing an injured knee— so, his plan was to take it easy, following us around all afternoon with camera in hand, filming our tricks.

Excited, we skied to the top of the terrain park, expecting to see a set of pristine, man-made jumps—but, the jumps were closed for maintenance.

Well, that was it for Lukas—he collapsed in on himself. I saw the enthusiasm fade in his eyes, his next words confirming what I hoped wouldn't happen. "That's it," he said. "I'm not going to compete . . ."

Lukas was a last chance qualifier for the contest, granting him the wild card title. Understandably, he was nervous—but, after not training successfully and not feeling prepared, he wasn't mentally ready to take on the event. Add the fact the jumps were closed?

The last straw.

"Lukas, you can—you'll be ready! I'll help you get there—and, you'll compete! If you put your skis on in the contest, and straight-line down the middle of the pipe? You'll still get more points from this event than you will from most of the other events we do this season combined!"

"I don't know . . ."

"You know you will because it's a World Cup contest! If you want to get a spot on the national team, you need to compete! You don't get handed World Cup spots like this every day . . ."

So, I came up with a plan to find somewhere on the mountain where we could take some air, and maybe even try some half-pipe tricks. Toward the bottom of the ski run there was a big pile of snow accumulated beside a man-made snow gun, stretching almost all the way across the run, and it looked like we could take it as a jump. "Careful," I warned as we approached. "The snow may be punchy, I'll go first . . ."

For the most part, man-made snow is pretty close to the real stuff. When temperatures drop below freezing and the gun is turned on full blast, it's like a micro blizzard. The snow piles up quickly—but, if the temperature changes slightly while the gun is on, the snow quality varies dramatically. It can land on the ground and be nice and fluffy—or, if temperatures rise and the snowflakes don't form, water molecules land on the ground, freezing instantly.

A problem.

The surface can look and feel firm, but, if skiers land heavily on their feet, they can 'punch' through to the soft snow underneath—which causes the skier to lose balance, and crash on landing.

"I'll go first," I repeated. My plan was to do a trick called a 360—one full rotation, taking off and landing forward. Simple. So simple, in fact, I used to call it a safety trick because I could land it every time on any jump.

With that in my mind, I set off down the hill toward the snowpile. In an instant, I was airborne, spun the full 360-degree rotation, and came down on my feet with a thud.

I landed it, and the boys skied behind me one after another. It was on, the session started, and we continued to hit the snowpile all afternoon. My plan?

It was working.

We were having fun, so we started our half-pipe tricks—back to the top after about four or five jumps each. I'll never forget standing at the top of the in-run to the snowpile, talking Lukas, Ty, and Garett through the tricks they were about to perform. Lukas was doing a trick called a 'Lincoln loop' which was a barrel roll similar to a downhill facing cartwheel in the air.

Ty planned a straight over back flip and Garett was performing a 720, the same trick as I—two full rotations, taking off and landing forward. I landed the 720 run before Garett, so, that time, it was his turn to go before me.

We went in order—Lukas first, and he stomped his trick! Then, Ty dropped in, laying out a beautiful back flip.

Stomped.

"Garett, your turn! Ante up, man!" I gave him the nod of approval, the obligatory 'fist-bump,' and he was off. He, too, landed it, nailing the 720, then skied away with authority. "Yes!"

My turn.

I set off down the hill, transitioning from my coaching hat to my skiing hat quickly. I remember composing myself mentally as I made my way down the in-run—my athletes had already gone, so, in my mind, I needed to catch up. *What trick am I doing? Oh, yeah—the 720. I've got this! I've done it a thousand times!*

I looked up—and, BOOM! Right in the mid-section— then, a sinking feeling. You know what I mean—my gut was telling me something. My instincts.

They were telling me something wasn't right.

I looked up, and it seemed Colin was standing with his camera right where I wanted to take off on the pile of snow, but he wasn't—it just felt like it. My inner dialogue, though, told me I needed to take off further to the left. *Whatever— it's only a big pile of snow. Besides, it's just a 720! I've done this thousands of times* . . .

A momentary lapse of judgment changing my life.

Forever.

I proceeded down the in-run, gaining speed toward the big pile of snow. I chose a new location on the snowpile to take off—slightly farther left—and, once I approached the pile, I knew it was a little bit steeper than where I jumped previously.

Good! The more air, the better!

I took off with the exhilaration and intoxicating rush that drew me to freestyle skiing in the first place and, once I was in the air, it felt automatic. I rotated fluidly, feeling my body micro-adjusting with ease, instinctively opening up for the landing. I extended my legs, like shock absorbing landing gear to catch myself when my skis met the ground.

Then, the catastrophic impact.

I'll never forget the noise—it was like a bomb went off.

I didn't know what was happening. I collided with the ground hard, but not on my feet as expected. My head and neck were thrust into the snow, and it felt like an upper cut to the face from a heavy-weight boxer. It was then I was aware of a sharp pain in my neck . . .

Then, nothing.

Uncontrollably I tumbled downhill, confused, as air in my lungs was all but lost. I tried to scream, but there was no sound—instantly, I knew.

It was serious.

For fifty feet, I rag-dolled down the hill, one ski coming off in the process. Finally, I slid to a stop, face down, supported by my other ski that wedged itself in the snow, my body weight pushing firmly against it.

My goggles slid down over my eyes, nose, and mouth, air returning to my lungs as I lay there, panting desperately. Panicking. All I could see was a thin band of light coming in the gap between my helmet and goggles, the lens immediately fogging up as I hyperventilated.

I couldn't get up. I couldn't roll over. I couldn't feel anything in my body.

"NO!! Noooooo! God, nooo!"

The weight of a thousand fists . . .

CHAPTER 3

INSPIRATION

As a young man growing up in Vernon, BC, Canada, I wanted more than anything to be an athlete. As it turned out, however, I was more of a wannabe than an athlete. From grade school until the time I was sixteen, I was a below-average student. I had heart, but heart wasn't enough when not making the team. In elementary school, I didn't make the volleyball team—so, in high school, I refocused and shifted gears. I made the basketball team, which was a big deal for me at the time, and it helped I was almost 6'2" in the eighth grade.

I'll never forget the moment I knew my basketball career was going places. I played center, and I loved winning jump balls, getting physical, blocking bigger guys out of our house, rebounding, and putting points on the board.

In a pivotal game against a big rival team, I was playing as well as I usually did and, on an offensive play, I had my moment—but, things didn't go according to plan. Everyone was out of position, and I found myself wide open, outside the key, but inside the three-point line.

The ball landed in my hands and I caught it as if it were second nature, but I was in unfamiliar territory. I looked for passing options to my point and shooting guards, but they weren't there. I was the only one wide open with an opportunity to save the play.

It was my time.

I put up a beautiful jumper, releasing the ball with smooth follow through, and time slowed down as I watched my shot soar overhead, no doubt in my mind I did what my team needed. I knew I could shine for my team.

Even so, the ball connected with the top right corner of the backboard, bouncing like a projectile possessed, all the way to the sideline and out of bounds. The result? My talent wasn't enough to keep me on the basketball team, and it was a pivotal moment changing my life.

Maybe team sports weren't my thing.

In PE I routinely put up C+ performances during fitness testing until the tenth grade. I tried out for and made the rugby team in my senior year because, even though I didn't have good hands, I could run—and, I could kick. So, second string winger and last-resort fullback were enough for me.

While I didn't excel as the athlete I once dreamed of becoming—being the star player for my team—I found my niche elsewhere.

When I was a sophomore, my focus shifted, and I started to love sports in which I was in control of my own destiny. No coaches. No teammates. No one telling me I wasn't good enough.

It was all on me.

From that time on, I started to excel in sports when I could push my own limits and live at my edge—the place where fear, anxiety, nerves, growth, learning, adrenaline, and the magic of life . . . coexist.

Enthused and excited, I began to thrive in individual sports such as skiing and snowboarding, skateboarding and mountain biking, among others. Any time I found myself upside down, flipping and spinning, I was in my element.

The thrill and familiarity made sense, too—I grew up near a cliff diving mecca on Kalamalka lake called Rattlesnake Point in the provincial park behind my house. With hundreds of rocky outcroppings, ledges, and runways from which to jump, my crowning achievement in those days was diving out from the notoriously named cliff—9-1-1— laying out picture perfect front flips. I loved what I used to call 'two-ball' sports—those performed sacrificing life and limb for glory's sake.

In the winters from age nine to fourteen, my snowboard and I were inseparable. Compelled to join the cult sport because of its inherent nature—i.e., categorized by rebels and talented riders who didn't conform to societal norms—I found my fit until one day at Silver Star Mountain Resort in 2002.

The truth is I was tired of chasing my brother and his friends around the mountain on their skis. The mechanics of skiing versus snowboarding favor skiers in their ability to go places snowboarders can't—and, on two edges versus one, skiers have an advantage for cutting across hills, going places I couldn't on my board. I lost elevation faster than skiers and it was tough to keep up, following them across the slope. So, I decided to try on a pair of skis for the first time in five years.

I skied when I was very young, thanks to my mom and dad who were passionate about spending time at the ski hill in the winter time. My mom, Pippa, learned to ski while working in the French Alps as a chalet maid in her youth. My dad, Rob, grew up skiing British Columbia in the 1950's and '60's, using skis that towered overhead. Not to mention leather boots—plastic was a revolutionary technology, not yet mainstream in the skiing world. Still, they loved the sport.

From six to nine years old, I chased my parents around the mountain until I realized I could straight-line the ski runs, beating them to the bottom—who needs to turn? Even then, I didn't have much of a self-preservation gene in my body, and fear wasn't holding me back much to the dismay of my mom and dad.

When I got back on skis that day, trading my snowboard for a friend's skis, it was just like riding a bike. I hadn't forgotten the moves, edging with both feet, driving the tips of the skis downhill, feeling the crisp cold wind as I hit speeds I missed on my board. I could keep up! Just like that! I followed my brother, Anthony, who grew up in the ski racing program, not one to concede to the snowboarding craze. Unbeknownst to him, I idolized him for his skiing prowess.

So, we arrived at the biggest jump on the mountain, a tabletop in the terrain park with a kicker and landing separated by a thirty-to-forty-foot gap. I never cleared the jump on my board, so I watched Anthony as he approached.

Following his tracks in my mind, I witnessed his flawlessly executed jump—and, if seeing were believing, I knew I could do it.

Monkey see, monkey do.

With inspiration to carry me, I set off down the hill, heart pumping, gaining speed—more than ever before—I felt my skis lift off the snow, and I was airborne! I soared over the gap, landing in the same sweet spot as Anthony had before me. Talk about ecstatic! I just cleared the biggest jump on the mountain! On skis! From then on?

No turning back.

I went to our local ski shop the next day and traded in my snowboard, bindings, and boots so Anthony could get new skis and I could have his old pair. There was no doubt—I was hooked, and I knew at that moment I was a skier. I found it—my sport. That decision would be the greatest decision I ever made, shaping the rest of my life. The search for the flow state, adrenaline, adventure—it would grip me for years to come.

Well, as you might imagine, my lust for hitting jumps on my skis didn't stop after that day. I was more comfortable in the air on skis than I was doing other sports I loved. In 2003, after skiing for a full year on my own and improving my skills with many 'crash and burns,' I convinced my parents I needed help—someone who knew what he or she was doing to help me achieve my high-flying goals. So, I convinced my mom and dad to let me join the local freestyle ski club at Silver Star. After all, they held the keys to the best jump on the mountain at the time—a jump to which the freestyle club had exclusive rights. It was jumps like that pro skiers T.J. Schiller, Josh Bibby, Riley Leboe, Justin Dorey, Joe Schuster, and Mike Mertion were using to hone their skills.

And, I wanted to be in their club . . .

Shortly after, I signed up for the development team which entitled me to one day per week of coaching on the jump. On my first day as a member of the club, I knew I was in heaven, surrounded by other skiers just like me! Everyone was sending it!

The development team program was all I thought I needed at the time to keep on the progression path, but I quickly realized it wasn't for me. I was older than most of the kids on that team, and my skill level merited additional attention. By the end of the first day, I graduated onto the competitive team, thrust into the group of greats. While I was under-skilled in my opinion, one person saw potential in me . . .

Josh Dueck.

Head coach at the Silver Star Freestyle Ski Club, he pulled me up to ski with his team on my first day skiing with the club. He proved himself on the competitive circuit, competing for the BC mogul team, giving some of the greats a run for their money on the mogul course. Josh had piercings, a rebellious attitude, and a contagious stoke for the sport, and his energy and approach to the free-form sport of freestyle skiing felt familiar—just like the vibe I got from snowboarding.

It couldn't have been better.

Even so, at the end of my first day with the club, Josh sat me down in the brown-bag lunchroom where the club gathered to start and finish the day. "Go home," he ordered, "and ask your parents to cough up another $495 dollars in team fees . . ."

"Why?"

"So you can officially join the competitive team." Then, he paused. "Do you think they can pay that much money?"

"I don't know, but I'll damned well ask!"

"Okay—our first competition is in three weeks. Let's get you ready!"

I couldn't believe what I was hearing!

And, all I needed was the green light from Mom and Dad . . .

The caliber of skiers I found myself skiing alongside was incredible, each on a trajectory toward greatness. Everyone on the team dreamed of one day standing on top of the podium at the U.S. Open, X-Games, or maybe—one day—at the Olympics, and it was Josh giving me my chance.

At my first contest in big air, I placed fourth, just shy of a podium performance, my trend throughout the season. At every medal ceremony, I witnessed friends getting medals placed around their necks and, in some cases, winning paychecks! Although I knew I would get there one day, it still stung a little knowing I was coming up short.

Until the last contest of the year.

By the time the BC Provincial Championships rolled around, my hard work paid off. I earned bronze medals in big air and half-pipe, and my dreams were already starting to come true. The following year, I stood on the podium at every event in which I competed, stacking up hardware on the competition circuit.

Soon, however, the luster began to tarnish.

Between my junior and senior years of high school, I ended up rolling my ankle badly in a wakeboarding crash, tearing all ligaments supporting the arch of my foot—and, I broke my tibia in the process. I'd never been seriously hurt before, but I convinced myself it would only be a minor setback. After all, it was summertime, and I had the entire Fall season to heal and be ready for ski season.

I waited a full three weeks before I started walking and swimming again, or trying to do other sports—but, like any young man, patience wasn't yet a virtue I possessed.

My ankle was destroyed.

Doctors said the bone healed well enough I could put weight on it, but it was ligaments sustaining the most damage. Bottom line?

I should have waited longer.

Finally, ski season arrived, and I still couldn't run, jump, or twist—at least, not the same as I could before the accident. But, that wasn't holding me back! I learned to tape my ankle to support the deficient ligaments, and wedging my foot in a ski boot was like putting on a cast. Yes, I was back skiing, but nowhere close to one hundred percent.

Not surprisingly, during my senior year, my contest results suffered, but I still managed to land on the podium at the provincial level, qualifying for nationals. The way I figured it, nationals, big air, and half-pipe events would be my big break—if I skied well in those events, sponsorships and endorsements were waiting. Then?

A wrench.

The week before nationals, I reinjured my ankle—a recurring theme—and, although it wasn't hurt badly enough that I couldn't ski, I wasn't performing to my potential. Of course, I competed, skiing as hard as I could—but, it wasn't enough.

I missed the podium.

With fifth and sixth placings in big air and half-pipe, for the first time over the previous two years, my dreams of landing on top of the podium at the X Games began to waiver, and I finished the year with a heavy heart.

I didn't make it.

Forced to make a difficult decision following that winter season, I enrolled in university. The trajectory I was on changed, and I felt for the first time maybe the top of the podium wasn't for me.

School seemed a good consolation prize.

I was accepted to UBC for engineering in Vancouver, a far cry from my skiing dreams—but, I couldn't do it. I chose the middle ground, enrolling in the Bachelor of Business Administration degree program offered near my hometown by UBC Okanagan. In my mind, I could better parallel a business degree with skiing in future years.

In my first year of post-secondary, my ankle healed. Amazing! I was back to my old self, but a year older, stronger, and wiser. I skied over sixty days that year, starting to win local contests and rail jams. I was back! That year, every day on the mountain was a gift because I was healthy! But, there was something different—when I skied, I was thankful I was healthy at that particular moment because I knew it could be my last day of the season if I got hurt.

Going into second year of university, I planned to take the winter semester off, committing my time to competitive skiing once again, rejoining my teammates and friends who were still competing. That meant training and, on October 23, 2007, we had our first team trampoline training session of the fall. I arrived with my friends, and the vibe before the training session was electrifying. I never felt stronger, or more ready to fly!

The coaches unleashed us into the gymnastics club gym in what seemed like structured chaos. I decided to start my night by bounding off the trampoline into the foam pit.

I watched a couple of other guys go before me, until it was my turn. I bounced higher than I ever had, laying out a misty 540 into the foam pit, one flip with a half twist. I came down with picture-perfect precision into the pit, landing with my feet tight together, just like I'd done so many times off the cliffs at Rattlesnake Point—but, it wasn't the ideal strategy in a foam pit.

WHAM! I felt it immediately. I pin-holed through the foam, hitting the cement floor, bottoming out in the foam pit!

I hit with such force that I knew something was very wrong. My ankle was in agony, and all I could think was, "Not again!"

The coach supervising us at the time jumped to my rescue into the foam and, when I crawled out, I knew, as much as I didn't want to admit it, I broke my ankle.

My other ankle.

That day marked the end of my competitive skiing career. I missed three winters, my dreams of winning the X-Games or Olympics up in smoke. To sit out, watching my friends compete?

Absolutely devastating.

But, when one door closes, I had to trust another opens—and, it did. Freestyle ski coaching. While I couldn't be on the mountain skiing and competing, I could still be there skiing and inspiring. I could take my passion and expertise in the sport, passing it on to the next group of up-and-coming skiers at my home mountain. So, I began coaching the development and competitive programs at my home club.

I finished my business degree in the process, coaching my way through my education. When I graduated university with my bachelors degree, I was healthy again and, naturally, skiing was still my top priority. It was then I moved to Whistler to align my education with my passion, and it must have worked because, the following season, I was hired to coach and manage the high performance team in British Columbia. At only twenty-three years old, I was coaching some of the best skiers in the country!

After two years coaching at the provincial level, I moved up in the coaching world, coaching the top Canadian talent from each of the provinces offering half-pipe. My job was to put my athletes onto the Canadian Olympic ski team, and I was succeeding. Simon D'Artois, one of my early protégés, won the X-Games in 2014, and went on to ski in the 2018 Winter Olympics! Not only that, in 2019, he won a FIS Crystal Globe, the top accolade for skiers in the International Skiing Federation!

Cassie Sharpe carried on, earning the title of first female skier from Canada to take home half-pipe skiing gold in the 2018 Winter Olympics in PyeongChang, Korea. She's an Olympic champion! She won X-Games multiple times, and is still known as one of the most accomplished and decorated women skiers in the world.

Brendan Mackay is a current national team member, achieving bronze in the 2020 X-Games while tracking to compete at the highest level in the 2022 Winter Olympics. My new dream became coaching at the Olympics, representing Canada. If I couldn't stand on the podium, I could help other athletes get there. I loved my role helping athletes to achieve their dreams, one I held closely to my heart.

But, everything came crashing down.

Chapter 4

BACK TO MY FUTURE

They say during trauma or near-death experiences our life flashes before our eyes. True. My mind raced, searching my memory banks for a similar experience, instinctively in survival mode—but, there was none.

This was different.

But, once I knew I was paralyzed, the confusion subsided, and I was instantly aware of my accident's significance. My mind flooded with memories of Josh Dueck—my first ski coach who, in 2004, broke his back and became paralyzed from the waist down, shortly after getting me into the sport. I knew my consequence.

I knew I was in trouble.

I knew I needed to talk to Josh, but that would have to wait.

My mother's worst fear was I would break my back or neck, and she never hesitated to be vocal about it—still, supporting her son's passion out-weighed her fear. Of course, I'm forever grateful for the opportunities my parents gave me throughout my being a part of the sport I loved so much. But, in my mind? I selfishly took away their freedom to live out their years in retirement without a dependent son.

I knew I'd need them more than ever.

Then, I felt a shift! My face slid on the snow, thrusting me back into the present. One of my athletes clicked off my ski, causing my body to slide but a few inches. "Did you move me? Don't move me! I can't roll over! I can't get up! I need someone to hold me in C-Spine . . ." Fight or flight took over, and I decided to fight.

But, I knew it wasn't going to be a short-lived experience.

Acceptance after trauma is a funny and interesting thing—it's necessary to move forward, and I jumped to acceptance almost instantaneously because I knew I was the master of my own destiny. For one, I caused the crash, and I couldn't dwell on my emotional pain. I needed to fix the situation, my mind moving to what's next—and, my next words still surprise me. "Colin—my life is going to be so different. I'm probably going to have to go back to school. But, I don't even read books, man! My life has always been 90% skiing and 10% everything else!"

A dramatic shifting of the tides.

But, it wasn't time to worry about my education—I needed help, and impatience vied for control.

"Where's ski patrol," I asked.

"They're on their way," Colin assured me. Garett and Lucas went to get someone . . ."

Minutes later with all hands on deck, medics prepared to delicately roll me over to place me on a spine board as Colin remained at my side, holding my head until it was time. Before rolling me over, however, they had to straighten my arms, placing them beside my body.

"We're about to move your arms to get you ready for the flip and spine board," one of the ski patrolman informed me.

Instantly, I panicked. How could they move my arms without rolling me over? It felt as if my arms were crossed in front of me, underneath my body.

"Wait! Wait! We aren't ready," I yelled.

"We're about to move your right arm . . ."

"No!"

The ski patrolman and physician moved my right arm which lay extended on the snow above my head, my bicep practically touching my ear, blocking the light.

As soon as they moved my arm parallel to my body, in an instant, I could see. *Oh, man! This is really bad . . .*

I had no idea where my arms were—it felt as if they were crossed in front of my torso, but, when they moved my left arm into place, I felt inexplicable, shooting pain. There was no injury, but my brain perceived my arm was in agony.

Still face down, the doctor carefully put a neck collar in place, relieving Colin from holding my head and neck—finally, he could put on his gloves.

Ready to roll, they turned me over, placing me onto the spine board. After almost an hour of being face down in the snow, I could see the accident scene including my three athletes, Colin, and numerous ski patrollers standing over me.

The on-hill doctor wanted to administer morphine at the scene of the crash, but I argued against it. I wasn't in pain, I couldn't feel anything, and the momentary agony in my left arm subsided. "I don't want any drugs! I need to feel everything going on in my body, and don't want my head to be clouded by narcotics!"

They obliged and kept things moving, securing me to the spine board, lifting me onto the toboggan for the dreaded ride down the mountain. With the exception of the ski patrol guiding my sled, it was the first time I was alone with my thoughts, despair taking root. Again, I knew it wasn't a crash I'd simply walk-off—if I ever walked again.

I lay helpless and terrified of what they might tell me once I reached the hospital. But, unbelievably, I started giggling! Usually, when riding in one of the ski patrol toboggans, there's a debilitating pain of some sort—but, I couldn't feel anything. It was, by far, the worst injury I ever had, but I wasn't in pain.

I couldn't help but laugh at the irony.

Once at the medical clinic at the bottom of the mountain, they placed me on a hospital gurney—that's when my luck began to change. At Keystone Mountain Resort, they're prepared for cases like mine, so, before a chopper flew me to St. Anthony's hospital in Denver, they took preliminary x-rays, and inserted an IV line, as well as a catheter. Then, as they pulled off my ski clothes, I saw my arm.

It didn't look real.

Was it possible the arm I saw in my peripheral vision was mine? Severity of the situation sunk in a bit further, but I didn't have much time to think about it—the helicopter was minutes away.

The guys carried me out, carefully placing me in the chopper, greeting the Flight for Life team. A short time later, I landed on the roof of St. Anthony's Hospital in Denver, a tier one trauma facility which services the entire state for medical emergencies like mine. Immediately, they transported me to a self-contained trauma unit for hospital intake, imaging scans and, eventually, surgery.

It's interesting what I remember during that time, such as talking with the chaplain as well as a nurse who was filling out my paperwork. The chaplain attempted comforting me with prayer and her company, which I appreciated. Quiet for a while, I decided to speak up. "Do you know what the worst part about all this is," I asked.

The young, brunette nurse turned to me, smiling. "What?"

"I was supposed to go to the gym tonight!"

She burst out laughing only to be chastised by one of the doctors. "Stop laughing," he admonished. "This is not a funny matter . . ."

"Are you kidding? Don't take this moment away from me! I'm never that funny!"

More laughs from the nurse, and a slight giggle from the doctor. The drab mood started to lighten—if only it could've stayed that way.

Shortly after, I was rushed to imaging where I proceeded to have multiple head-to-toe x-rays, cat scans, and magnetic resonance imaging.

Headfirst, I spent 107 minutes in the MRI machine—the worst. My head was wedged into a plastic ring with foam squeezed in around it. As if feeling claustrophobic in my paralyzed body weren't enough, my head was tightly held in place by foam and towels, my body pushed headfirst into the magnetic resonance imaging machine, its ceiling hovering inches above my face.

The image tech who prepped me for the MRI made her best effort to insert ear plugs, but they held for just a moment before falling out. An MRI machine slammed magnets together, sending a resonating magnetic wave throughout my body, creating the image frames. Repetitious, loud, banging was the icing on the shit cake.

Before going in, the tech prepared me regarding what to expect. "You'll be in there for a while—if you need help, push this button . . ." Then, she placed a small, handheld button on my torso, hurrying out of the room.

Was that some kind of sick joke? I couldn't move a thing!

Regardless, I went in for the MRI and, after a few minutes, I couldn't take it. I remember yelling at the top of my lungs—again, not loudly because my diaphragm was semi-paralyzed.

I came out of the machine only to be informed I moved, so we needed to repeat the procedure—the largest portion of my spine—for twenty-seven minutes. The good news was I might have moved, even though I was calling bullshit on that—the bad news was I was in a lot of pain.

Finally, I asked for drugs. "Knock me out," I requested. "I don't want to be awake for this anymore . . ."

Things were turning dark, tears streaming down my face.

When the imaging was complete, I met with my surgeon, Dr. Thomas Puschak. He towered over me at six feet four—a big man with an even bigger heart. The Croatian blood running through his veins bestows an innate ability for caring for his people, and I'm incredibly lucky he came to my rescue. His compassion and confidence comforted me, and I knew I was safe in his hands.

Shortly after our first meeting, I was off to surgery— four hours on the operating room table during which time Dr. Puschak installed two titanium rods and ten screws, fusing five vertebrae in my neck. He cut away all the bone from around my spinal cord after realigning my neck, giving my spinal cord room to swell without impingement, its only hope for physical recovery.

Finally, it was over.

As unbelievable as it might seem, my successful surgery proved to be a pivotal moment—a catalyst—setting me on a trajectory I could have only imagined at the time.

Chapter 5

REALITY

—DAY 1, DECEMBER 17th—

When I awakened from surgery, I could bend my elbows slightly, intense relief flooding through me when I realized I could move something.

No longer was I fully paralyzed.

Although I had a lot to learn about quadriplegia, in my mind, I was good! Things were looking up! Something changed and, maybe, they'd keep changing! But, in reality, I was far from good—just because I could move my elbows didn't mean the journey would be easy—or, that I'd ever walk again, or have any kind of independence.

Colin, a few of my athletes, and their parents were at the hospital without my knowledge. Colin ended up sleeping at the head of my bed after I was admitted to the intensive care unit. I imagine he made that decision so I wouldn't have to be alone when I woke up in a foreign, sterile environment. It says a lot about his character, doesn't it? He was there for me and, with some of my athletes' parents, I had people to lean on for help.

Hearing me stir, Colin walked around the side of my bed, groggy, still in his ski gear. Sleeping in that particular chair could have left anyone paralyzed after a night of being kinked up! He may have been feeling worse for the wear, but there was no way he'd let me know it.

As you can imagine, we talked about what happened— you know, how it all went down, and he filled me in on the crash details. We even watched the video. Then, he told me the surgical procedure—a posterior laminectomy fusion of five vertebrae—was successful, and the doctors said I might recover, but there were no guarantees.

Suddenly, my mind jumped to my family. "Okay—I should call my parents, and tell them what happened." Then, I noticed the look on Colin's face. "Colin! Did you tell them already?"

"Man, your mom and stepdad are already on their way down here. We couldn't get a hold of your dad, so we had to call your mom. There was no way they were letting me sign all your paperwork for the surgery without talking to your parents first . . ."

Right then, I wasn't sure what to think—in my mind, it was better to wait until I knew exactly what was going on before I called my mom. No one wants to receive a phone call like that, and she received a few on my behalf in the past. I understood why they needed to call, but damn it! I knew her worst fears had come true!

I had no choice—I asked Colin to call her, putting it on speaker. I couldn't hold the phone, let alone press the button to turn it on, and dragging a lifeless hand across a touch screen probably wouldn't help much, either.

Mom answered. Although my memory of the words we exchanged is foggy—yet, on a chemical cocktail of meds at the time, I remember one thing . . .

Her love and tears.

I listened as she cried, her voice tearful, but reassuring—she and Barry, my stepdad, were on their way.

Then, I tried to call my dad who was in Mexico at the time with his partner, but they couldn't be reached. Next in line for a call should have been my brother, Anthony, but he would have to wait . . .

I needed to talk to Josh.

I didn't know it then, but the call I made to him altered the trajectory of my entire life. Often, we don't appreciate what can take place in a matter of moments—or, in the heat of the moment—until much later. I knew it was an important call to make—after all, Josh was someone I idolized, respected, and loved. He had also been in a wheelchair for about ten years at that time.

Fortunately, he answered, his words and guidance bestowed over the following few minutes, I'll never forget. "Mike," he said, "you've just been inducted into the spinal cord injury club. It's the most elite club in the world—and, you're going to meet some of the most incredible people, and have some of the most incredible experiences.

But let's be clear, no one wants an invitation to the spinal cord injury club—spinal cord injury is devastating, and I wouldn't wish it on my worst enemy. However, there are good things that can come from it—it just depends on how you look at it." He paused for a second, his words sinking in. "Although it doesn't feel like a gift right now, there will be gifts that reveal themselves over time . . ."

I'll never forget Josh's leveling with me. He didn't know what it was like to be a quadriplegic—he was paralyzed from the waste down with full use of his arms, hands, and most of his abdominal muscles. But, he did know I wasn't in for an easy ride, confirming conclusions I was already making.

As real as our conversation was, he gave me light.

I remember thinking it's about gifts and perspective . . .

There will be gifts.

I was on board with that idea, and immediately started searching for and looking forward to such gifts to come. In fact, I felt the immediate perspective shift I already experienced was a gift.

On the first day, it took no time at all for me to recognize what was important in life and what I'd been ignorantly taking for granted—health, happiness, and my loved ones. Time is the most valuable thing we have and take for granted on a regular basis. Everyone is always in such a hurry to get things done and move forward that we often miss out on the magic of the moment.

When my body was ripped away from me in an instant one day earlier, it took with it my independence and identity. I would have killed to have picked my own nose once that ability was gone—thank goodness for Colin's help! And, of course, my mom, who stepped in to manage much of my personal care forty-eight hours after the crash. She was always on my phone and taking care of my social media, connecting me with the outside world. My stepdad, Barry, was tirelessly sorting out insurance, the air ambulance, and everything in between—both were there for me when it mattered most.

I realized almost instantaneously what was important in life, and what I took for granted was a gift—and, I never had that kind of perspective in my life.

So, I made it through the first day without much anguish, all the while wondering if it were just a bad dream. But, for the most part, I was dealing with my new reality fairly well. It helped I was surrounded by people who cared for me.

—DAY 2, DECEMBER 18th—

I awakened on the second day, groggy after a restless night. Excruciating pain set in overnight making sleep an elusive prospect—so, I lay awake wondering if my bad dream would ever be over. Shortly after I ate breakfast, however, I faced the realization my bad dream would become my reality for the foreseeable future.

Two men stood at the end of my bed, both in white lab coats with stethoscopes garnishing their necks, clipboards in hand. One was tall with dark features, his clean cut, well-groomed goatee giving the impression he was a practiced medical professional. I recognized him—he was my spinal surgeon who operated on me just two nights prior.

The other gentleman, a bit smaller, had platinum white hair with a wispy white mustache. To me, he looked like the oldest thing in the hospital—which probably wasn't a stretch because I was in a modern medical trauma center. He was the spinal specialist who saw more cases like mine come through the hospital doors than anyone.

Quietly, they were discussing my charts, reviewing intricacies of my surgery. Prior, we discussed the procedure to fuse five vertebrae in my neck from my third cervical vertebrae to my seventh—it was my only hope for physical recovery.

Of course, I eagerly awaited their assessment.

The man with the white mustache lowered his tone. "Mike, you've had a very severe spinal cord injury. The bones in your neck shifted in such a way, they compromised the spinal cord causing so much damage no signals are getting through to the lower extremities in your body."

"But . . . I can move my arms! That has to be a good sign, right?"

"It is a good sign—but, the level at which you hurt your cord wouldn't have affected the mobility we're seeing. The movement pattern we observe is in line with what we expect to see for your level of injury. Nerves protruding from your C4 and C5 vertebrae control the muscle groups you're currently accessing in your arms and shoulders . . ."

At the time, I could only shrug my shoulders a bit, engaging my deltoids to lift my arms off of my body ever so slightly. I could barely close my elbows, meaning my biceps were working, but I needed gravity to help the elbow flop open.

I had no triceps function.

"Mike," the spinal specialist continued, his voice serious. "You should prepare yourself because you'll probably never walk again."

His words sank in for a moment.

"What? How do *you* know? I mean . . . how do you know?" The strength of my words surprised even me.

"Every vertebral junction in the spine has neuropathways which deliver messages to your body. The level of your injury so high in your neck means the movement you're experiencing is due to healthy nerve pathways above the injury. Everything below remains paralyzed . . ." He looked to his partner, the surgeon, for a validating nod.

"I don't know if you're right," I said, my comment greeted with a surprised look. "I mean, what if it keeps changing? My arms are working, and they weren't before the surgery. So, things could keep changing." I hesitated, considering I may be in denial. "I hear you—I'll listen to your words, but I don't want to jump to that conclusion right now. I think I'm going to wait and see . . ."

I knew he could be right. I couldn't move anything below my shoulders and biceps—but, I wasn't about to let a person I just met tell me what the rest of my life held. Especially when the prognosis wasn't something I wanted to hear. I listened, but I told myself I'd be open to the possibility I could—and, would—heal.

I prepared myself for *that* reality.

Promising myself I'd do the mental and emotional work to accept my future as a quadriplegic—if he were right—I still wasn't settling for his diagnosis and prognosis.

Here's the thing—the only person who knows what you're capable of is you. I'd soon learn we're capable of more than we think, and we can do more than we think we can do—and, in that moment, I felt I was capable of healing. I can't explain it, but I had a feeling they were wrong. Maybe I was being a bit stubborn, but, I wasn't about to let two men—whom I just met—define *my* possibilities for the rest of my life.

In that moment, I didn't feel I would just walk again, I felt as if I would ski. I probably wouldn't ski like I used to, hitting big jumps and doing flips, but I did see myself skiing wide open, forgiving, fluid, powder turns. I didn't practice formal visualization in that moment, but . . .

I saw myself skiing.

What's weird is if someone would have asked me if I'd ever ski again, in that moment I would've said, "Absolutely!" I knew in my heart it might not be possible, but I had to try—and, I knew admitting defeat wouldn't help me get to where I needed to go.

I held onto the idea my arms were moving.

Something changed.

I had hope.

—DAY 3, DECEMBER 19th—

Again, I awakened in the middle of the night to nurses entering my room so they could turn me from one side to the other. There was a high risk of pressure sores on my skin, due to paralysis and inactivity, so I needed to shift every couple of hours. Not pleasant. But, it was part of the new reality I faced.

The nurses turned me over, propping my body up using numerous pillows until I was borderline comfortable, and drifted off to sleep.

The next time I awakened, it wasn't to nurses—I simply drifted out of sleep and reached up, touching the neck brace which I hated. Scanning the room, I could see lights flashing on my heart rate monitor—my resting heart rate was low, below forty beats per minute, which concerned my medical team. I assured them, however, it was normal for me.

I'd never been in such good shape in my life as when I had my accident. For healing purposes, that was a good thing—but, it was hard knowing I was likely going to lose all of my muscle mass to atrophy.

Glancing at monitors, tubes connecting me to the I.V. bag, my wound's blood drainage, and catheter?

I couldn't believe I was there.

Still in disbelief, I turned my attention to my body. Every waking moment, I tried sending messages to it for movement, or any activity below my injury. If only I could wiggle my toes! But, they weren't responsive. So, I figured I'd try something different.

I sent the message. *Move, legs!*

Nothing.

I tried again. *Move!*

Then, again and again. The sensation was different each time—I couldn't put my finger on it, but I knew something was changing. I tried again and, as though my body were coming back to life, I felt something shift.

No way! Again!

I sent the message to my legs to lift off the bed, and I heard the stiff bed sheets crinkle. I couldn't feel it, but I was pretty sure I was moving my legs! I tried again and again. My body was shifting!

I shouted to Colin, whom I knew would still be sleeping at the head of my bed in that awful chair which offered little comfort in such a dire situation. "Colin! Wake up! Are you there?"

Colin sprang to action, landing on his feet beside my bed. "What's up? What's wrong? Are you okay?"

"Turn the light on! Turn the light on! And, can you sit me up?"

Colin turned on the light, then used the hospital bed's controller to sit me upright. My legs slowly came into view as the bed ascended, the neck brace and titanium rods making it impossible to tilt my head. I tried to move my legs again—but, they were non-responsive.

Was I dreaming? I swear they just moved!

"I think I can move my legs . . ." And, in that instant, my right knee shifted ever so slightly upward.

The left took a bit more convincing, but it, too, lifted an inch or two off the mattress. "Colin! I'm moving my legs! I'm moving my legs!"

Colin just started screaming, "You're moving your legs! You're moving your legs! Weeeeooooooh!!"

Naturally, with the ruckus, my nurse ran into the room. "What's going on here?" All was quiet in the intensive care unit aside from our hollers.

"He's moving his legs," Colin told her. "He's moving his legs!" He hugged her, and she joined in the celebration, cheering for joy.

But, the victory dance was short-lived as she hushed our cheers. "Shhhh! This is amazing, but we need to keep it down!"

"Okay," I said with a grin. "This is just unbelievable!"

It was unbelievable—less than twenty-four hours prior, doctors told me I'd never walk again, and there I was moving my legs! In my mind, I knew things were going to be okay.

From that moment on, I was 'good.'

Of course, I was far from good, but I knew I could get better. That moment in my dark, ICU hospital room poured fuel on the fire of hope—it would be my possibility. I would walk again. I would ski again!

The timing was perfect—I moved my legs the night before my family was due to arrive at the hospital. One of my biggest fears was seeing my mother's tears for the first time. My dad, stepdad, and brother would all put on a brave face, but I knew my actions had devastating consequences for my family.

The words 'family first' couldn't be more accurate in my situation. There's a ripple effect for all of our actions and, in my case, the first ripple—the aftershock—was felt by my family. But, I had good news, and I could give them hope, assuring them everything would be fine.

I didn't think of it at the time, but there's a reason some say ignorance is bliss. I wasn't fully aware of the work I needed to put in over the coming weeks, months, and years to make my vision a reality. I wasn't aware of my proceeding struggle . . .

But, I was off to a good start.

—DAY 4, DECEMBER 20th—

The sensational celebration was short-lived. I was happy and grateful my legs could move ever so slightly, but I wasn't out of the water.

I realized quickly there were many more complications to my spinal cord injury.

I couldn't feel anything in my body, and I had no idea if I needed to go to the bathroom. I had no idea if I were hot or cold. I couldn't even tell if my legs were on the bed, or touching the floor. I felt pain—a good thing in some regard because it alerted my body I needed to alter my position. But, the pain in my neck was becoming intolerable, and my doctors kept upping my narcotic doses.

On a rotation of Valium, hydro-morphine, dellodid, Tylenol 3s, percocet's, gabapentin, bacolophen, oxycontin, and oxycodone, my mind and body were in a daze when I felt the narcotics take effect. Opioids were taking ahold of me, and I had no control—but, I needed them to numb my pain receptors.

It was unbearable.

I couldn't access any of the muscles in my torso. Nurses tried to sit me up at the side of my bed, but my body was like a sack of rice. When tipped to one side, there was nothing stopping me from slumping all the way over onto the bed. When upright, it was all I could do to keep myself from fainting because my blood pressure dropped off a cliff.

I couldn't control my ankles or toes—only the large muscles in my legs while my wrists and hands remained lifeless.

Friends thoughtfully brought me Christmas presents during their visits, but I didn't have the dexterity to unwrap them let alone enjoy them. It was mentally and emotionally draining, but I kept smiling, knowing it would help me in the long run.

—DAY 5, DECEMBER 21st—

I couldn't wait to see the spinal specialist, wispy mustache and all. When he arrived in my room, I greeted him with a huge smile.

"I hear you have some good news to share with me," his tone a 180 from our first encounter just days before. "Show me what you can do!"

I started moving my legs, showing him I wasn't going to take my situation lying down. I could lift both knees a few inches off the bed, and I was more confident with my intentional movement. And, I could lift both legs at once, or I could alternate. I could even do it to the beat of the joyous music playing inside my head.

Well, the specialist was astounded, and his words lifted me up. "Nurse! Nurse!"

My nurse arrived quickly, looking at both of us. "Yes?"

"Did you know this man can move his legs?"

"Yes . . ."

"Well, what are we waiting for? Let's stand him up!"

In that moment, the spinal specialist became my new favorite ally.

—DAY 9, DECEMBER 25th—

A team of physiotherapists and nurses gathered around, planning the logistics of my big move. It was the day I would stand up—and, it was only fitting it was Christmas Day. My mom stood poised to film the big shift on her phone's camera. We unintentionally documented every day since the accident, and that day would be a worthy memory to capture.

Everyone took position, assuming their respective roles of the well-choreographed transfer. My medical team was planning to move me into a wheelchair, so I could get rolled out of the ICU to the step-down spinal unit—and, to make the transfer, they would stand me up in the process. I couldn't wait, although none of us knew how it would go.

None of us knew if I would be successful. "Okay, Mike— I'm filming," Mom commented, pushing the button on her phone.

With one physiotherapist supporting my back and two others holding me by my sides, we prepared to make the move.

My feet were on the floor, but I couldn't feel it. Polished tiles should have felt cool to the touch, so I asked if it were cause for concern. "I can't feel anything, so how will I know if I'm doing it or not?"

"We'll be here to support you all the way, and we'll catch you if you fall." He paused. "Are you still willing to try?"

"Absolutely!"

With my feet planted firmly on the floor, in one big push, I was upright! It was my first time standing up at 6′2″ in nine days, and it was terrifying! I couldn't tell if I were squeezing my muscles or not, and my knees completely locked out—so, it were as if I were standing on stilts.

The physios urged me to move my feet so I could pivot, turn 90 degrees, and sit down in the wheelchair they had staged for me—but, no such luck.

I couldn't move my legs, at all.

I was frozen, putting all of my effort into supporting my weight. Standing used to happen automatically, without intention . . .

Then, it seemed so foreign.

Chapter 6

AFTERMATH

Long travel days aren't fun for anyone, even if you have your own private Leer jet. It's less fun when enduring two separate ambulance rides fastened firmly to a spine board on top of a three-hour flight. Thankfully, my mom was with me for the journey. Her strength in those moments became my strength.

Being unloaded from the air ambulance and arriving in Vancouver felt like a blessing, and a curse. I was making progress. I knew I was closer to home, and one big step closer to taking back my life—but, mentally?

Things were definitely getting worse before they were getting better.

The rug was pulled out from under me—my reality and the severity of the devastating injury I experienced was becoming blatantly clear.

My hospital room at Vancouver General Hospital shared space with three other patients. I didn't have roommates in Colorado, and I didn't have to share my nurses—understandably, I think, my comfort level dropped, and so did my spirits. I tried to cling to strands of hope and gratitude I had left, but I was beginning to crack.

I lay in my hospital bed at night, alone with my thoughts, the faint sound of my heart rate monitor constant. *If I can get my arms to work properly, I'll rip out this I.V.*, I thought. *But, I'll be more careful of my wound's blood drainage hose and, for sure, my catheter . . . but, I'm going to smash that heart-rate monitor!*

Then, I mentally replayed the spinal specialist's words in my head. "Mike, with intense physical therapy, you might get back the use of your arms. But, prepare yourself—you'll probably never walk again."

That's when I lost it. I cried, and cried—my ribs should've hurt from the heaving sobs, but I couldn't feel it!

I can't even feed myself! I can't even wipe away my own tears! Life, as I know it is over . . .

It was then I questioned who I was—Mike Shaw the skier? Athlete? Coach?

Will I ever have kids? A family? Probably not . . .

My future—every dream—was gone, and there was no bouncing back. No guarantees.

I was a quadriplegic.

I survived the night, awakening the next day realizing once again it wasn't a bad dream. I was still there, lying in bed, ready for it to be over. I wanted my old life back, and I knew . . .

The honeymoon was over.

I remember talking with my dad that morning. "This was never part of the plan . . ."

"What do you mean?"

"Well, you don't grow up a dreamer, thinking about what your life will be like, thinking that one day you'll grow up to be in a wheelchair. It's never part of the plan . . ."

In that moment, my dad's wisdom and cool headedness shone through. "We don't always get out of life what we think we're going to," he advised. "You're right—some things just don't go according to plan, and it's unfair. The trials and tribulations we face in moments like this might alter our path, but it's also the moments like these—the tests—that can change us for the better."

"What do you mean?"

"It's our challenges like this making us who we are— they define our character. They alter our course, and, in the process, make us grow and adapt . . ."

I lay in silence, digesting his words.

"Some things," he continued, "will never be the same. But, some things will be better for it. I've already seen a change in you—in your perspective—that's quite remarkable."

His words helped, but it didn't mean it was going to be easy.

During bad times? It's normal to go to dark places in our minds. We know we aren't where we're *supposed* to be—but, I couldn't help it. As far as I was concerned, the life I lived— everything I knew to be real in this world—was gone.

I'd be lying if I said the words 'why me' didn't enter my thoughts. I couldn't help but wonder why it happened to me when so many of my friends and people I knew in skiing were taking bigger risks than I. It wasn't fair!

But, such thoughts weren't serving me.

It took effort, but, when those thoughts came into my mind, I let them drift out as surely as they'd come. Beyond the clouds is always blue sky, but, sometimes, cloud cover blocks the sun.

In time, I learned to call that place the dark pit. My rock bottom. In the dark pit, I couldn't get any lower—I was so deep in depression and despair, it felt as if I could pound my fists on bedrock, the gates of hell, and it wouldn't make a difference.

Everything was dark. A struggle. A place I loathed.

From my hospital bed's vantage point, I could see tops of buildings as I looked out my room's small window. In January, Vancouver is as gloomy as I was at the time, and seeing the sun is a rare treat amid endless strings of rainy days. In the distance, I saw snow-capped mountains, their presence bringing comfort—and, cruelty.

I longed to be there.

I missed the mountain air and joy of skiing more than I could imagine.

Even so, there was a bright side to being in Vancouver. Aside from being home in Canada, enjoying the healthcare I had access to—my right as a taxpayer—I had my community. As soon as I arrived, I was inundated with visitors, my closest friends and family at my side as soon as I lay my head to rest in the hospital bed at VGH. My closest friends stayed the night on the small, back-breaking furniture in the corner of my room. Friends whom I hadn't seen since high school walked through the door, and the small windowsill began to fill with cards, treats, and toys.

At one point, I recall lying down with friends surrounding me, attempting to eat grapes and fuzzy peach candies—but, of course, I couldn't feed myself. My hands were unresponsive to my commands even though I tried to pinch or pull individual grapes off the vine. Sometimes, I had enough strength to pop the grape off the vine, only to have it skip across the hospital room floor. It looked clean enough, but there was no way anyone was eating the hospital room floor grapes. I struggled to smile until a fleeting thought drifted in . . .

I have grapes! I have candies!

Not only that, I had people who cared about me enough to feed me grapes and candy. *I'm in a Canadian hospital with medical care and attention. I'm not in pain—much pain anyway. I'm here. I'm so lucky.*

And, it was true. The support I had, plus the good fortune of being where I was at a time when there were medical support systems in place for someone in my position was a miracle.

I was thankful for the fact I would survive.

My life would go on regardless of my physical abilities. Honestly? If my injury happened in another time or another place, I might not have been so lucky.

My physiotherapist at VGH was a woman by the name of Hilary—and, Hilary was a gift. A New Zealand ex-pat living in Seattle and working in Canada, she was stubborn and committed to my success, never taking no for an answer while motivating me to move forward.

On my third or fourth day under her care, she decided I needed to get back on my feet. After the first time, I was anxious as well as fearful—as much as I wanted to get back on my feet, the thought of being upright and out of control was intimidating. "Right," she said, assessing the situation. "I think it's time we got you up and out of that chair, don't you?"

"What? Today? Are you kidding? Am I ready?" I hesitated for only a second. "I mean . . . of course, I'm ready!"

"Of course, you're ready—you've been sitting around all week since you arrived here!"

"Absolutely! Let's go for a run while we're at it!" I couldn't help laughing!

So, Hilary took the reins, moving my chair into position in front of a set of parallel bars, and a walking path. She and her assistant moved a ceiling lift into place with a sling attachment that looked like a fancy jolly jumper for adults. Positioning the harness around each of my legs, she fastened the belt around my waist, then attached it to the ceiling lift.

It was time for me to try standing upright.

After a couple of weeks of inactivity, atrophy was causing my wrists to curl upwards and my fingers to curl in toward my palms uncontrollably, even though I had plastic braces to prevent it from happening. Wrist guards worked to keep my hands' condition from getting worse, but they made it next to impossible for me to grip the parallel bars. In order to make the lift successful, I was going to have to fully engage my legs.

When the time came to stand up and I was in the right position, Hilary moved in front of me. She came close to me, crouching down with her shoulder pressed firmly against my chest.

"Are you going to do a fireman carry? What's going on?"

"Don't be silly! You have to do the work—and, give it everything you've got. When we say go, you need to push up on your legs with all your might!" A brief pause. "1-2-3—push!"

In a moment of maximum exertion from Hilary and me, I vaulted upward. I was standing again! The ceiling lift and sling slowly wound up, catching up to me a full six feet off the floor. When I felt the tension, my fear immediately dissipated.

Unlike the first time I stood in Denver, I took in the view, enjoying the feeling of being upright. I wore my hair in a samurai-style bun, appropriate for the moment as I felt like a warrior. In that moment, I was in the dojo, training, fighting for my life. Stakes were high—if I were to succeed at regaining control, strength, feeling, and coordination in my body, I might be able to enjoy some of the activities I lost in my life. If I failed? I would have to adjust my plan, but I couldn't go there just yet. Failure wasn't an option, and it was a fight I had to win.

"Well done, Mike," Hilary shouted. "Keep your quads flexed, and keep squeezing your butt muscles! Try to keep equal weight on each foot . . ." A lot to think about as she prodded my quadriceps and glutes.

I couldn't contain myself! "Oh, my god! This feels unreal! Do I walk on them?" I was, of course, referring to my legs.

"Oh, no—not yet! You have to stand before you walk, Buddy!"

The victory was as fleeting as it was monumental. I stood for about a minute before I began to feel faint, as though I would pass out standing up. Unbeknownst to me, my blood pressure was all out of whack because of my spinal cord injury—the spinal cord is an integral part of the central nervous system helping regulate blood pressure. In my case, my blood pressure spiraled, making me feel dizzy and faint.

Standing for the second time was a big step forward in my recovery, but it didn't come without a certain caveat—in order to move over to G.F. Strong, the rehabilitation hospital, I would have to maintain an upright standing position for over five minutes. The rehab facility is intended for patients who are stabilized, ready for an intensive rehabilitation program. I wasn't there yet, and one minute wasn't going to cut it.

The next day in physiotherapy, we tested my tolerance in an upright position using a standing frame, unlike the first time when we use a jolly jumper, and I had to use Hilary as support. This time, the standing frame braced my legs in place and, by pumping a hydraulic ram, I could slowly crank the seat upward and forward until I stood upright.

I needed to show everyone I could be upright for five minutes if I wanted to move to the rehab facility—and, I was determined. There was, after all, a lot on the line. We were informed at Vancouver General Hospital there was a bed at G.F. Strong open within the week and, if I could hold the standing position for the required duration—five minutes—I was a good candidate for the bed. Now, keep in mind, those beds weren't available frequently. The fact one was available during my first week at VGH was unique since people often spend weeks or months in the hospital before moving to rehab.

All I had to do was stand for five minutes.

I made my way into the standing frame with Hilary's help, as well as her assistant. The transfer from my wheelchair to the standing machine wasn't graceful—I hadn't practiced any transfers aside from moving back and forth from my bed, which was done using a ceiling lift and sling. But, we did it—someone cranked the hand pump, inching me closer to the upright position.

As soon as I was vertical, I knew it felt better than the previous time I tried standing. *I've got this!*

The timer started. I could see it in front of me, ticking away. Seconds added up quickly, then the minutes. I was comfortable and confident until the three minute mark approached—then, the seconds started slowing down, and the next minute couldn't come fast enough. *Four minutes, almost!*

I started to pass out.

Fortunately, Hilary noticed, releasing the pressure on the hydraulic ram, causing a quick descent to the seated position. I didn't lose consciousness, but I knew I failed the test. I would have to do better if I were to make it to G.F. Strong any time soon—and, at that point, I didn't know how soon it would be.

Two days later, I awakened to learn two representatives from the rehab facility were coming to gauge my readiness for advancement to G.F. Strong. It was fantastic news, and a huge step in the right direction.

At the regular hospital, I was surrounded by people who weren't in the same head space as I. In my mind, there was no question I was getting better with every minute, but there were people around me in the hospital who not only lacked that common mindset, they were also physically deteriorating. The amount of 'code blues' I heard over the intercom, referring to a patient experiencing cardiac arrest, was humbling to say the least.

I needed to move.

The two people from G.F. Strong were amazing, their positive energy palpable and, as soon as I met them, I knew where I needed to be. I passed all necessary requirements in terms of moving onto the next phase of my recovery except for two—the standing test, and I needed to test my bladder function. I was connected to an indwelling catheter for three weeks, so going to the washroom was something I hadn't even thought of at that point. But, I couldn't stay catheterized forever, so it needed to come out.

I decided bladder first.

The following morning, I knew I was getting my catheter removed. I don't know if you've ever had a tube inserted all the way up your urethra into your bladder, but it's an intrusive experience, whether the tube is getting inserted or removed. I wasn't looking forward to it and, worse, I was scared. What if I couldn't pee?

Well, if I couldn't pee, I would need to use intermittent catheters every three hours, or every time I took in more than 16 ounces of fluids—which isn't very much. That meant every time I wanted to pee, I would need to shove a hose into my penis until it reached my bladder, draining the reservoir.

Not fun.

My dad was my rock, and I remember our conversation before the procedure took place. "Mike, what happens . . . happens. I know you're scared of what could happen—not being able to go on your own—but, this is the next step. Hope your bladder will work, and take the necessary next steps to fix the situation if you learn it doesn't."

I knew I could rely on his consistency and strength, his words offering those traits to me. My mom wore her heart on her sleeve from the moment she learned of my injury, relying on others for strength, sharing her grief. My dad, however, appeared more stable, unaffected by my accident at the surface level.

So, with Dad's advice to carry me, I moved onto the next step. A nurse arrived, tasked with removing the indwelling catheter. After explaining the procedure, she removed my clothes, exposing the hose. Carefully, she started to pull the hose out. After three weeks, it had become part of my body and, when it moved the first minuscule amount, a sharp pain shot through my body making my abdomen convulse uncontrollably. She kept the momentum going as the remaining several inches of the hose withdrew. My body went into a brief spasm as the muscles surrounding my pelvic floor convulsed. Thankfully, after a few moments of my body's reacting, it subsided.

It was done.

Then, we waited. I had a maximum of three hours before the nurse returned with a machine to test my bladder capacity. If she saw my bladder was full and I hadn't peed on my own, I'd need to be re-catheterized to drain the urine in my bladder. The new catheter would only be temporary, removed after my bladder emptied. If I couldn't pee on my own in three hours, that would be the process I'd need to repeat every three hours until my bladder regained function—*if* my bladder regained function.

The waiting game . . .

After three weeks, I still had little to no feeling in my body from my chest down. I couldn't tell where my legs were, at all—they could be straight, or contorted like pretzels. They could be on or off the bed, and I would have no idea. I had no proprioception—the awareness of movement, equilibrium, and balance. All I could feel was pain, which was a good thing. Pain is a great indicator that something in your body isn't right, and you need to make an adjustment, or solve the problem causing the pain. For balance, coordination, and movement, proprioception is a necessity.

Two hours passed. I was drinking water like it was going out of style to swell my bladder to a point where it might burst if I didn't relieve the pressure.

Then, two-and-a-half hours.

I had no inkling I needed to pee. I kept prodding and applying pressure to my lower abdomen, but there was nothing. My apprehension started to climb.

Two hours and fifty minutes.

My nurse returned to check on me. She wheeled in the ultra sound machine, as well as a tray with towels and jelly used to create the fluid contact with my skin to produce the ultra sound image. Alongside the jelly lay two catheters about eighteen inches long, one of which would be inserted into my bladder if I couldn't pee on my own.

"Any sensation you need to go yet," she asked.

"No—not yet. Can we wait a few more minutes? Do you have any waterfall, or bubbling brook music I can play?"

"No," she laughed. "But, for you, I can wait a few more minutes. I'll be back . . ."

She left the room, leaving me with a pee jug and an encouraging smile. Then, my dad came back, telling me to relax and let my body do its thing.

Wise words.

I shut my eyes, sending all of my intention to my bladder. I let everything go. I let go of the thought it might not happen. I let go of my worry it might not happen. I let go of the tension I was holding. Stress is a good primer when the going gets tough—but, sometimes, we need to release its grip on our bodies to let things flow.

And, flow they did.

Immediately, it felt as if I were bursting at the seams— which I probably was after drinking a half gallon of water. "Quick, Dad! Pass me the pee jug! I think it's happening!"

He placed the pee jug in my lap, and I positioned it in place in the nick of time—I almost completely emptied my bladder! An exhaustive 16 ounces of urine filled the jug, and I was elated!

I never thought I would celebrate taking a pee with my dad with so much enthusiasm in my mid-twenties. He probably hadn't been that excited about my peeing since the first time I didn't pee all over the bathroom floor during potty training. Nevertheless, it was a victory well worth the accolade.

Relief coursed through me—I felt it at a cellular level, and the emotional ecstasy came in waves like I never experienced. But, I didn't have time to think about that—I had other obstacles to overcome.

That afternoon, I was scheduled for the standing test.

It was the deal breaker or deal maker—what would determine whether I'd be granted a bed at G.F. Strong. But, with newfound courage and confidence from my victory in the morning, I knew I could manage the challenge.

Sometimes, it's important to take stock, reflecting on our wins. For me, it was easy to focus on how much I couldn't do, or the areas where I wasn't winning because there were a lot of them. I still couldn't take care of myself, and the idea of walking this thing off seemed an insurmountable challenge. Out of reach.

However, I could pee! I could do one thing for myself, and that was a drastic improvement from where I was only moments earlier. Once in a while, we need to celebrate small victories, building ourselves up. Our beliefs stand in the way of our success more than anything, and building self-confidence to know we have what it takes to win will help us get out of our own way.

I went into the standing test that afternoon not hoping, but knowing, I'd succeed. I transferred into the standing frame, helped pump the hand crank to get myself to an upright position, and the timer began to tick.

I watched the stopwatch in front of me tally second after second until it was minute after minute. I approached the four-minute mark and felt strong—until my vision started to fade. I could see glimpses of bright light and darkness in my peripherals. *No! I have to hold strong!*

I took a few deep, intentional breaths, keeping my attention on the stopwatch. Four minutes. My awareness returned, and acknowledged my peripherals. I looked around the room, my eyes meeting the representative from the G.F. Strong rehab facility who was administering the test. I knew I'd done it.

I fought through the dizziness, careful not to exhibit signs of duress, until the five-minute alarm chimed.

I won!

What a day! I went from feeling fear, anxiety, and the
unknown in the morning to feeling elated, successful, and
strong in the afternoon. All of us experience days like that—
when our mindset changes depending on the day. Heck, it
can change depending on the hour, sometimes the minute.
Celebrating our small victories can be fuel on the fire burning
inside all of us to do more—and, be more—than we think.

Chapter 7

WHEN YOU MAKE PROGRESS, KEEP MOVING

—Day 21, Moving Day—

My medical team might have felt momentum from my two wins the previous day because they processed my transfer to the rehab hospital quickly. While it might have been the fact I was making such great progress, I suspect it was due to the lack of available hospital beds. Either way, we weren't wasting any time, and I was eager to move on. Only three weeks to the day since my crash, I was moving onward and upward, following the same curve as my healing trajectory straight to the rehab hospital.

For the transfer, I was strategically dressed in an adult diaper and the standard issue hospital gown—for obvious reasons. I was still at risk of soiling my underwear, so it was a necessary precaution—moving from one hospital to the other involved a transfer from my bed to the ambulance gurney, getting wheeled out of the hospital and loaded into the ambulance, a short drive to the rehab facility a handful of city-blocks away, and being wheeled inside.

As soon as I got inside G.F. Strong, I could feel it— the energy was different. There were bulletin boards with all sorts of positive messages, posters, and pictures on the walls, and the intake staff greeted me with enthusiasm and warmth. I was in a place where healing and taking back life was the number one priority.

Wheeled into my room on the third floor where I was transferred into my new bed, as quickly as they dropped me off, I was alone, sitting upright. Scanning the room, it was refreshing to see walls were a rich yellow, the green sconces creating a lush glow—no more sterile grays.

A breath of fresh air.

Near my bed—no doubt left by the previous occupant— there were two small, one-pound dumbbells on the counter, and 'welcome' was posted on the wall. I had my own bathroom, and the light shining in through the giant window made it seem as if I moved into my own personal studio-suite apartment.

But, as I took it all in, I began to feel faint. My temperature shot up through the roof and I began to flush, causing me to worry I was going to pass out. What was wrong? I wasn't even standing upright!

Later, I learned I experienced autonomic dysreflexia, a quadriplegic's defense mechanism when something in his or her body is wrong. Autonomic dysreflexia can result from something as simple as a full bladder, or something as severe as my foot being folded over itself inside of my boot—I'd really have to use extreme force to get my boot on and fold my foot in half—but, you get what I mean.

Frantically, I tore at my hospital gown because I needed to cool down—easier said than done when I couldn't use my hands. I fumbled with the gown, using my wrists and hands to move it aside.

Once exposed, I saw the most horrendous sight—what was probably causing my incredible discomfort and light-headedness. In shock and horror, I looked down to see the most unbearably deep-front wedgie I'd ever seen. It looked like someone gripped the front of my diaper, and pulled as hard as they could up my stomach.

With all the activity that day, shifting and sliding around in the ambulance as well as gurney transfers, my diaper climbed its way up into the creases of my groin. The skin around my hip creases was bright red—it *had* to be what was causing my discomfort and dizziness.

I thought to call my nurse, but better judgment caused me to try on my own. I fumbled around, my lifeless hands of little use at that point, and I couldn't grip the sticky tabs on either side of the diaper to relieve the pressure. I eventually worked my fingers inside the waist band, wedging my hands farther and farther into the diaper.

With all my might, I pushed my arms into it, levering my forearms outward until—pop! The plastic sticky tab on the left side of the diaper released! I could feel the cooling sensation flood across my skin and my dizziness subside almost immediately, but not completely.

I wasn't out of the water.

I started on the other plastic sticky tab, but because the tension was released on the other side, I couldn't get it off. I couldn't take the diaper out of my hip creases, and I needed help.

Carefully, I covered myself back up after hitting the nurse-call button attached to the bed rail—I could hit it with my elbow. Almost immediately, the nurse came in—Kathleen. Petite and blonde, she was about my age.

"I need some help," I said after a quick introduction.

She responded in a concerned tone, "What's wrong? How can I help?"

"I just . . . I just need you to help me with this . . ." I thought for a moment about a more detailed response, but couldn't find the words. How could I describe a diaper front wedgie in a way it would be believable? So, I decided to show her my struggle. I pulled back my hospital gown to expose my dire diaper trauma.

"Oh, my God! I see! One second . . ."

As she was reaching for my diaper, I clumsily pushed the left side of my diaper across the front unintentionally, fully exposing myself to her. I looked down with a massive smile on my face—I couldn't believe it! I had an erection! As if spring loaded, it was all of a sudden standing at attention, full mast. I must have stirred it up while fumbling with my diaper!

It had been three weeks since seeing any life in that part of my body. I looked up at Kathleen with nothing but jovial joy on my face.

The glare she returned didn't match my enthusiasm. "I guess I'll come back when you've calmed down . . ."

It occurred to me, I just asked for her to 'help me with this,' then showed her my penis. I couldn't believe it!

She walked out of the room.

Well, my moment of elation quickly deflated due to my sense of urgency to remedy my dire diaper problem. I hammered my elbow against the nurse-call button.

Kathleen came in without the same candor she entered with the first time. "I'm so sorry," I said. "I didn't mean to—but, I really, *really* need your help! I can't get this stupid diaper out of my crotch . . ."

"Okay, okay . . ." With a good yank on the diaper, she removed it completely.

"Oh, my God . . . thank you." Relief swept over me almost instantly as the skin around my groin could once again breath. "And, I'm so sorry. I didn't mean to do that . . ."

"It's okay. Really . . ."

"No—I really didn't mean to do that. It wasn't the first impression I was going for, and I definitely don't want to be known as the 'Boner Guy' . . ."

"Mike—it's okay! These things happen, and it wouldn't be such a bad thing to be known as the 'Boner Guy' on this ward . . ."

Words I'll never forget.

She left the room, leaving me with a stone-cold realization—after a spinal cord injury, most patients don't have proper bowel, bladder, or sexual function.

In my past life, I took all of the above for granted. I didn't think about going to the washroom—and, luckily for most people, sexual function happens naturally. The satisfaction we experience from a healthy functioning bladder, bowel, and genitals is something we certainly wouldn't take for granted if we thought about it—but, the reality is most people don't think about it. Such naturally occurring phenomena takes place in our bodies for as long as we can remember—so, why would it trigger us as something we take for granted?

It wouldn't.

It probably wouldn't even show up as a small blip on the radar of the things we think we take for granted.

Alone in my room, I realized I had much to be thankful for even though I lost so much—and, I might be known as the Boner Guy on the spinal cord injury ward.

A title I would have happily accepted.

By late afternoon, the dust settling from the diaper incident, my family arrived, and I had a couple of friends drop in to visit. Together, we prepared to go for dinner in the common area at the spinal cord injury hospital ward.

Things were moving quickly in the rehab facility. They transferred me into a power wheelchair for dinner, the chair issued to me by the occupational therapy team that afternoon. I wasn't cleared to drive it on my own, but I could drive under supervision, riding along while one of my nurses controlled the joystick.

While breakfast in bed is pretty cool, breakfast, lunch, and dinner in bed gets pretty old when it's all you have. The freedom of the chair meant by dinnertime, I was ready to eat my first meal sitting upright in three weeks.

I wheeled into the common room which was a good-sized space with a long table in the middle. There were no chairs at the table—wheelchair parking only.

Shortly after I entered, it started to fill with other residents on the floor. I hadn't thought about it before, but I realized quickly spinal cord injuries come in all shapes and sizes. There were people with less neuropathic function than I, and some with far more. There were paraplegics—paralyzed from the waist down—and, there were quadriplegics, paralyzed from the neck down. There were incomplete and complete injuries in the room, meaning some people had incomplete neuropathic function below the level of their injuries, while others had none.

So, while eating dinner with my parents and one or two friends, I attempted to feed myself. I learned to pinch my pointer finger and thumb together by squeezing my whole hand—kind of like a misplaced lobster claw thing. I gave it a valiant effort with the utensils, but that wasn't happening even with adaptive grip aids.

On to Plan B—I tried picking up food by hand, but, once I collected the food in my fingers, getting it into my mouth was a target I just couldn't hit. Good thing I was wearing an adult-sized bib!

I was making progress in healing, that's for sure, but it had only been a day or two since I could lift my arms high enough to scratch an itch on my nose. I still couldn't touch the top of my head because my arms and shoulders were too weak to get them that high.

The struggle was real, but I made it through my first meal sitting upright, and it felt good! Up to that point, the first day at G.F. Strong was an absolute blessing, more uplifting than I could have imagined . . .

And, the best was yet to come.

After the first day, I was thoroughly exhausted, but there was one thing I needed to do to get myself ready for bed—brush my pearly whites. I usually did it from bed with the help of a nurse, a wash tub, and a bottle of water—it had been quite a while since I controlled the brush.

My nurse decided I should brush my own teeth, and I was all for it. I watched as she attached a foam grip to my toothbrush, quintupling the diameter of the regular brush—handy for lobster claw grip.

Mom applied the toothpaste, turning the faucet on for me once I got my grip on the brush. I wetted the brush, inserted it into my mouth, and started to brush—luckily, I had better accuracy than I did at dinner!

I didn't have the wrist dexterity to maneuver the brush from tooth to tooth, so I used my tongue for that. My arm and hand helped with the back and forth motion, and I was laser focused on getting the job done when something amazing happened.

I started to cry . . .

It was the first time since the day it happened, I did anything—and, I mean anything—for myself. I hadn't even picked my nose on my own yet. The loss of my independence weighed heavily on me for the twenty-one days leading to that moment—but, right then, I knew I could take care of one of my self-care routines.

Never in my wildest dreams did I imagine feeling such profound gratitude for something as trivial as brushing my teeth. Doing so definitely didn't show up on the radar of things I thought I took for granted—it's something I did every day, not giving it a second thought. You know—a compulsory activity I had to do.

In that moment, I was crying tears of joy because I could brush my own teeth.

The reality is we don't truly appreciate the wonderfully unassuming activities we have in our lives, or the great things our bodies automatically do for us on a daily basis—until they're taken from us. It's possible to feel grateful for such things, but it takes mindful intention to take awareness there.

By the time I was ready for bed, I realized I finished the day feeling full of gratitude, as well as full of a renewed sense of motivation to take back my independence—and, my life. There was nowhere to go from there, but up.

Or, so I thought . . .

Chapter 8

STRUGGLE

—Day 24 - January 10—

We were playing board games in the rehab hospital's cafeteria on my third evening at G.F. Strong when it happened—within the first two days, I received the 'all clear' by my occupational therapist to pilot my power wheelchair on my own. What a liberating freedom! All I had to do was place my hand on a metal cradle attached to the chair's joystick controller, and boom! It was just like playing real life Mario Cart.

The control I had over my arms must have been improving because I successfully passed the driver's test by steering the heavy unit around the hallways, through doorways, and in tight places—all without crushing anyone's toes or breaking any legs.

Everything was going so well, I felt up to having a group of friends over on a Friday night to play Settlers of Catan, a favorite game at the time. It gets pretty competitive when trying to take over the world, especially with the high-flying skiers I had as friends.

There were eight of us—I had the largest chair of course, weighing in at over three-hundred pounds, four-fifty if you included me on it. Getting the power wheelchair close to the table without hitting the joystick the wrong way and running it over was a challenge, but I made it work.

Our group included professional skiers, snowboarders, base jumpers, sky divers, a D.J., a cinematographer, an Olympian, an insurance broker, and a couple of other awesome, great friends who drove down to Vancouver from Whistler, where I was living at the time of my accident. I was finally surrounded by my community, and it felt amazing!

With their help, I learned to squeeze a plastic drink bottle between my hands, taking a drink on my own for the first time. Things were going so well, it felt as if I had a critical piece of my life back, my conscious mind releasing the pain and suffering that plagued my mind all hours of the day for but a few moments.

Everyone laughing and joking, time flew, and I hadn't been up and out of bed for that many consecutive hours since my accident. I was exhausted, but I couldn't help but give my all to my friends who were there for me.

I was in a good position to win the game, but I needed help, of course. Braden moved my pieces around the board and held the playing cards for me, but the strategy was all mine. Braden was the professional snowboarder, sky diver, and base jumper in the group—he was and still is one of my best friends. We're a year apart, both of us growing up in the

Okanagan valley, not far from one another, doing the same kinds of sports. When I moved to Whistler, he and I clicked immediately.

After my turn passed and Braden made the moves on the board, I realized I had to pee. "Want to rip upstairs with me? It'll only be a couple of minutes, and I could use your help with the elevator . . ."

"Sure, no problem . . ." As usual, he was always there for me.

I knew I didn't have much time, the sensation in my bladder growing urgent. Braden pushed the button to open the elevator for me and, once inside, he had a chance to ask how I was doing. "Man, really—how's it going? You look like you're doing awesome!"

"I'm doing pretty well, everything considered. It's a brutal injury, and I'm scared—but, I think it's going to be okay. Today—tonight, really—is the first time I forgot about how bad things actually are since it happened."

"Dude! That's so good to hear! Everyone is so pumped for you to get better, and be back in action!"

"I am, too—I don't know how long it will take, but it's all up from here." The elevator doors opened, and I drove my rig out into the hallway. "My room is right over here. Easier to use the bathroom in there . . ."

We set off down the corridor, entered my room, and I got ready to take a leak. At the time, I was wearing loose fitting gym shorts for easy access—I definitely wasn't standing to pee, and transferring onto the toilet from my wheelchair for a good old-fashioned sit-down pee wasn't in my repertoire yet. So, I figured out how to pee into a plastic jug while sitting in my wheelchair.

I pulled up my shorts on the right leg, held the pee jug in place, and managed to lobster claw myself into position, so I would surely send the stream of urine into the receptacle. Once ready, I relaxed, allowing the flow to commence.

As I started peeing and heard the jug filling as it was supposed to, I started to feel something unusual. I couldn't quite tell what was happening. *Is it? Am I? No!!!*

I'm pooping!

I wasn't just emptying my bladder, I proceeded to completely unload into my wheelchair, and I was helpless to prevent it from happening. I writhed around trying to do something about it, but the effort was futile. I sheepishly finished my pee, placed the jug on the counter, and got ready to roll back out into the room.

The door was cracked the whole time, but I could tell Braden was none the wiser as to what just happened. "Braden, will you do me a favor and call my nurse, please?"

"Sure, why, what's going on? Anything I can help with?"

"Just the nurse would be fine—please, man."

"No problem, are you sure I can't do anything for you though?"

"Yup—just the nurse." I said with a bit more malcontent. "You can tell her clean up on aisle two . . ."

I still don't know if it were the words or the smell, but he got the picture. With an expression on his face signaling he knew exactly what I needed, he exited the room quickly, only to return moments later with the nurse, and another helper.

"Thanks man, but you probably don't want to stick around for this . . ."

With his nod, I knew he clearly understood. "I'll wait downstairs." Immediately, I felt as if the rug were pulled out from underneath me. My mind flooded with the embarrassing scenarios unfolding downstairs as all of my friends heard I shit myself in my wheelchair. I felt flushed, anxious, and panicky, and I would have done anything to get out of my own body at that moment. *Why did this have to happen? Why did I ever have to try that trick that day? Why me?*

My nurses proceeded to wrap a sling around me while I sat in a pool of my own feces. They used the ceiling lift and sling to lift me out of the wheelchair, then swing me over top of my bed where they'd carefully laid out a plethora of sanitary pads. Once lying down on my back, they could start undressing me. When all of my clothes were off and I was lying there naked, one of the nurses took my clothes. "I'll package these up, and send them off to the laundry straight away . . ."

"Are you kidding? That's okay—just burn those!"

Humor, I learned, is a great way of masking suffering.

Nurses continued cleaning me up, applied diaper rash cream, and dressed me. This time, I was wearing a diaper. It took a while to get a clean cushion for my wheelchair because it was after hours, and all of the occupational therapists were off duty, but my nurses figured it out. By the time I wheeled back down to the cafeteria where my friends were waiting, it had been my turn to play for fifty-seven minutes.

My skin was crawling, my mind racing. I never felt so small, ashamed, or vulnerable in my entire life. My injury was tearing me up from the inside out—I lost so much already and, right then, I lost control. I couldn't control the most basic body function—something to which most people don't give a second thought.

It just happens.

What would girls think? They'd probably be grossed out. But, the chances of my having a girlfriend again were slim, anyway—I could barely pee, let alone have sex. And, even if I could, my abs didn't work, and my bowel could erupt at any moment.

My guy friends? They'd probably laugh at me, and be more understanding—or, they'd forget about it faster. Even so, I had to go back to face them because I knew they were waiting for me.

I drove my wheelchair around the corner, entering the cafeteria, rolling up to the group. I took a leap, facing my fears. "Sorry, guys! Guess I pooped myself!" I had to come right out and say it—otherwise, it would keep eating at me. I figured it was the only play I had—after all, they probably heard all about it from Braden, anyway.

"Yeah, we know! We've been waiting—it's your turn!" Jamie, my friend since one of my first trips to Whistler and never one to hold back from calling a spade a spade, can come off as abrasive, but she's one of the most compassionate people I know. It was her compassion deescalating the situation in my mind with only a few words, and I'd never been more grateful for friends like them.

They waited for me for over an hour, the game on pause, until I came back. They were there for me. They were my community.

My team.

As I drove the power wheelchair slowly across the cafeteria, my skin started to crawl, and my mind was racing. My feelings of anxiety and despair were directly proportionate to the risk of embarrassment to which I was exposing myself. There's a correlation between the potential consequences of our actions, and our reluctance to take the next step. In my situation, I found no other option but to take a step forward—figuratively speaking—embracing my fears, pushing through them. I had to lean into the feeling of discomfort, persisting beyond my stress threshold. I'd never done anything like it before in my past life—it wasn't me.

As a kid growing up, I felt vulnerable on the playground. I worried about what people thought of me, and I wouldn't take risks or put myself out there for fear of rejection—and, I paid the price. Routinely, I was picked on, and singled out by my peers as someone weak. I was bullied and, at times, it was relentless.

In high school, once I started playing team sports, I was never the star. I wouldn't try to take the winning shot because it might be the losing shot if I missed. I wouldn't take the shots because I could fail—and, I preferred to be average, blending in, because the success of the team was never riding on me. I didn't talk to my crush because she might have thought I wasn't cool enough, or worthy of her time. I let my fear of failure in the social constructs of life curtail my ability to achieve as much as my potential offered.

Vulnerability paralyzed me well before my accident ever did.

The only sport giving me self-confidence, as well as the wherewithal to take risks, fail, and pick myself up again was freestyle skiing. Maybe it was because winning or losing was all on me since I didn't rely on a team—I was more willing to take risks. But, the reality is skiing is very much a team sport. We relied on each other, and we supported each other when I started out as a young competitor. It was like no other sport I experienced at that time—when people I competed against were also my biggest supporters.

My teammates.

Most teams we're a part of are like my old ski team. In most cases, the people around us—our teammates—are there to pick us up when we get knocked down. They're the people who embrace our, stress, fears, and vulnerabilities so we can fully live at our respective edges, pushing the envelope, and pushing the needle toward a better tomorrow.

It's important to know we have support. Our supporters won't always be there when we need to take a risk or to push our limits, but they'll be there if we fall. They'll be there to pick us back up, so we can try again.

Vulnerability, I learned, is in the mind. It's a restrictive mindset disabling us far more than any physical restrictions ever will. We can't be afraid to take risks, fail, fall, or collapse. It's where so much learning, growth, progress, and magic of life exists—in that space where we're living at our edge, embracing the unknown.

When I wheeled back up to the table, my mind was running rampant with the same kind of thoughts holding me back in my life prior to having a spinal cord injury. When faced with no other options but to move through that feeling, I learned a valuable lesson.

When we feel vulnerable and fear, stress, and anxiety accompany our vulnerabilities? They're indicative of growth, progress, and success we can achieve if we take the next step forward. Moving into our vulnerabilities is an absolute must—if we don't, we're depriving ourselves of much of the human experience making us feel truly alive.

When I heard my friends' words, I received their support. They were there to pick me up after I'd been knocked down because they were simply there—and, trust me, I was down. Again, I'd never been that vulnerable. It may have seemed trivial to them, which, sure, it probably was—I was building it up in my own head. I mean, how can a person really judge me in a situation like that where I'm a recent quadriplegic who shits his pants? Yes, it sucks—but, do they think less of me? Absolutely not! They accepted me with empathy, helping me accept my vulnerabilities, as well as accept my setbacks, showing me the way forward.

My perspective shift in that moment made the majority of lessons I learned in life pale by comparison.

Your team—the people around you, as well as your community—will do the same for you. If you think they might not? Well, it means they're not your people.

Take a leap, let yourself be vulnerable. If your team comes back with overwhelming support, you know they're there for you. If they don't, know they just gave you a gift. Our willingness to embrace the unknown, fear, anxiety, and our emotional exposure keeping us paralyzed gives us freedom to blaze new trails. Those who might throw our vulnerabilities back at us are those who liberate us, providing the opportunity for growth.

Perhaps, more than we'll ever know.

It may be difficult, but all of us need to find our communities—we need to find people who lift us up like my friends at the board game night.

That night, I learned, vulnerability wasn't my weakness, but, in vulnerability lay my capacity for courage. Being vulnerable wasn't being weak—being vulnerable became my strength.

In those few moments, I grew immeasurably as a person.

Chapter 9

A DAY IN THE LIFE . . .

At twelve, three, and six in the morning, nurses came into my room to turn me over, giving a top up on my meds, if needed. Because my arms weren't strong enough and my abdominals weren't cooperating, I needed help shifting my body back and forth from side to side. After a while, I got used to the nurses' manhandling and, most times, I didn't fully wake up. It was a routine comfort when they shoved pillows underneath my body, propping me up toward one side or the other.

Sleeping pills, oxycontin, and oxycodone were effective, so I typically awakened to breakfast either being placed on the bed tray, or to a cold plate of food after an early morning delivery. Breakfast in bed administered by my attending nurse was a blessing, but the humility required to accept mouthfuls of food from a stranger tested my patience. Over time, though, I hoped to get better at helping myself.

After breakfast, it was time to get out of bed. Every other day, I went through the bowel routine. If that were the case, my nurse would lift me out of bed using the ceiling sling, then place me on the commode—a tall wheelchair with an opening under my bum so it can wheel over top of a toilet. Once in position, wearing my stylish hospital gown, I sat—and, waited.

Sometimes, I was lucky—things moved quickly. Other times? Not so much. I couldn't push, so the stool in my colon and rectum would only move if I got my ratio of laxatives right the previous day. Fortunately, my nurse helped if too much time passed, and nothing happened. Digital stimulation was a thing of beauty when I was backed up—which I was.

My nurse, Susan, a Filipino grandmother who sang to me in my room every morning, bringing much delight, looked up at me from her crouched position on the floor beside the commode chair and toilet. With lubricant on her gloved fingers, she was ready. "Okay, Mike—I'm going to do the digital stimulation now."

"Just one? Let's try two today, don't you think, Susie?"

Laughing, she proceeded to do her job. "Okay—here goes!" Her head ducked down as she attempted to get things moving, resurfacing moments later. "Oh, no, Honey—it's hard. Really hard. I'm going to have to dig . . ."

I'll never forget the hook-like motion she made with her finger as she glared up at me, her face riddled with concern. Right then?

I would have given anything to be somewhere else.

Humor was all but gone from the situation. "Do what you have to do, Susie."

She dug and dug, trying to relieve my constipation. As I looked down, I saw a steady stream of blood trickling into the toilet. But before long, it was over, and Susie cleaned me up.

Making my way back into my room, I felt utterly deflated and exhausted. Then, she lifted me out of the commode chair, putting me back in bed. It was much easier for Susie to dress me when I was lying down—once she selected my outfit, making sure I was dressed to impress, it was time to start my day. It only took two hours—and, it wasn't even my shower day.

They were every three days.

Next thing on my schedule was physiotherapy. Luckily, my nurses gave me extra oxycodone in my morning dose, so I could try to get through it with as little pain as possible. In physio, I was working on moving my wrists, as well as repetitive motion to gain more control and, sometimes, I isolated larger muscles and joints in my body. My priority was to learn to live with my disability, strengthening areas showing signs of recovery.

After physio, it was time for lunch—back up to the spinal ward in the hospital where I ate the daily sandwich special. It wasn't pretty, but I ate everything I could to fuel my body's recovery.

In the afternoon, I sometimes went to hand therapy learning to pick up pennies out of buckets of sand, or try to feel the edges of a die. It was frustrating when I couldn't complete the tasks—but, the truth was there were other quadriplegics around me with electrodes attached to their hands, desperately hoping for a flicker of life in their thumbs and fingers.

I also went to wheelchair skills class, where it became apparent the world isn't made for them. It was there I learned how to transfer from a wheelchair to and from a bench, or maybe a car. I even learned how to navigate a crosswalk, or the wheelchair ramp outside of my local drugstore.

There was also occupational therapy where I had help with adaptive utensils, learning how to cook a meal without full arm or hand function. Not only that, I learned how to get in and out of a bathtub, as well as how to transfer onto a toilet by myself—all the while hoping, of course, I could actually go to the restroom without another set of helping hands one day—which looked unlikely.

Some days, there were meetings with wheelchair reps, their job to meet recently injured paras and quadriplegics in the hospital to sell them their first wheelchair. I needed to be careful with my selection because my wheelchair became my legs, carrying me some of the places I used to go.

It had to fit well.

But, if I were lucky, it was wheelchair sports day, and I went to the gym to participate or watch the other patients perform an awkward display of athleticism. As quirky as it sounds, it was the highlight of my day! But, sports and passions sliced like a double-edged sword—activities capable of making me feel on top of the world were also capable of cutting me down.

I would have killed to have my old body, and athletic abilities back.

The only thing that could have been better was getting in the rehab hospital pool—but, rules stated I couldn't have had an accident for three weeks to gain access. For me, it was only a matter of days since I shit myself, so it was out of the question.

Usually, by the time I made it back to my room, I was exhausted. If I wanted to go back to bed, it meant I had to ask my nurse to use the ceiling lift to transfer me. Sometimes, I transferred several times a day—but, around dinnertime?

I toughed it out.

My fatigue would have been more tolerable if only it weren't accompanied by unbearable pain. Thankfully, my second daily dose of opioids would start to take effect—the drugs made me lethargic, but they were a necessity, and I couldn't handle therapy without them.

A highlight was visitors—while nothing changes inside the hospital, everyone else's lives keep going outside of it. They shared their news, and I shared mine with my Groundhog Day stuck on repeat. I had to tell the story of my crash many times, reliving the moment with each new visitor.

After dinner—a serving of meatloaf and creamed corn, bland chicken stir-fry, or something similar—I was eager to get back to bed. But, I had to wait my turn because everyone on the spinal ward had the same idea, and I could hear call switches sounding off around the ward. When the nurse arrived to help me into bed, my new roommate, an older gentleman, took priority. Actually, I hadn't talked much to him, probably because I felt a bit of his resentment because he hadn't moved anything below his waist.

Once my head landed on the pillow, I felt an incredible sense of relief. The only time I wasn't in pain was when I was horizontal, and I had the right pillows supporting my body and neck. The neck brace was itchy, but there was nothing I could do about it, so I tried to push it out of my mind.

By then, it was only seven-thirty, so I watched a movie if I had one downloaded on my computer, but the nurse had to set it up for me. Usually?

I didn't have the energy, and I dozed off.

Invariably, I awakened to the urgent sensation of having to pee. Luckily, the pee-jug was within reach, and I took care of it—then, I called the nurse to collect and empty the jug. If I didn't want to get out of bed one more time with the ceiling lift, she helped me brush my teeth in bed. Once done?

Time to attach my condom catheter and pee bag.

It required application of a condom using medical grade glue which was attached to a hose, and clear plastic bag. Since I couldn't get up during the night and using a pee jug was too risky in the dark, I peed into the condom catheter. It was better than an indwelling catheter, but I always had to hope there weren't any leaks. If the tube were kinked, the condom could turn into a dreadfully misplaced water balloon—only when it popped, it wasn't water inside.

Finally, bedtime.

Just me, my neighbor, and the darkness. I hated that time of day—you know, after my last visitor left and my last bit of attention was from the nursing staff. Just me, my limp body, and my thoughts.

Can you imagine?

Doesn't sound like fun, right?

But, that's how it was—days like that were common, and long nights were the worst.

I had a name for those times—the long, dark nights when I was left alone with my thoughts. You may remember the place I call the dark pit. I tried not to go there, but, sometimes, I couldn't help it. I went to that place in my mind when, up to this point, I haven't shared with more than a few people who were close to me. Now I'm sharing it with the world!

Go figure . . .

I used to write about the dark pit—well, I told Siri what to write for me on my iPhone. I articulated the dark pit in a note to myself . . .

"The dark pit—spinal cord injury is the deepest, darkest pit you will ever be in. However, the lessons you learn can be applied to everything in life, be it relationship distress, other injuries, or financial distress—anything where you feel like desperation is present.

Overcoming something like this lets me know I can overcome anything challenging in my life. It's a lesson for everyone—the process is the same to overcome the darkness from any distress. You have to understand what has happened, put it behind you, move forward and come up with a plan to get yourself out of the pit."

The dark pit embodies the deepest, darkest, depression I ever felt. I compared my spinal cord injury to death, disease, and heartbreak. Sometimes?

It would have been easier if I were just gone.

I still have that note on my phone from February 11, 2014. I used to talk myself out of the pit routinely because I had to—I couldn't be so distressed and depressed, hoping to heal the way I wanted and needed. So, I had to figure out a new plan.

I needed to figure out a new way out of that head space. Besides, there was—and, always is—a lot to live for. I had things to look forward to . . .

When faced with a seemingly insurmountable obstacle, an adversity absolutely not part of your plan, what do you do? Do you crumble? Admit defeat?

Or, do you try to maintain an objective perspective, approaching the problem with poise and purpose?

One thing was certain—meals in the hospital weren't five-star dining. Still, I never felt more grateful for bad coffee in my life than while I was within the walls of G.F. Strong. My morning coffee was something I looked forward to every day, and that small bit of normalcy—pleasure—went a long way.

Some mornings, my bowel routine never went according to plan, and there were times in physiotherapy when I couldn't get through the session because my pain was too severe. During those times, however, I grew most. I never thought I'd need intrusive help to go to the washroom, and I didn't want to be in pain. Neither were part of the plan—but, when something in life throws a curveball, all of us have the power to adjust our perspectives.

Your perspective is how you see and understand the events unfolding around you. It's how you see things in life that happen to you. You may have heard this phrase, "things don't happen to you, they happen for you." It's about perspective. To take control of our outcomes and prevent being overwhelmed by emotion, choose objectivity and gratitude.

What do I mean? Try looking at your situation with a level head. Try to find the silver linings and the opportunities for learning, growth, and advantage. Things happen to all of us, fair and unfair—but, how we react dictates whether we will succeed by turning tragedy into triumph. Or, whether we lose control of our emotions, miring ourselves in fear, despair, and powerlessness.

How we choose to react is interesting—I recall being completely frustrated during a hand therapy session one afternoon. I was aggravated because I couldn't feel anything in my fingers—until I took a look around me. When I surveyed the room, there were plenty of other patients who would have killed to have the opportunities I was getting. Yes, my finer dexterity was all but gone, but I was starting to get movement back. I could pinch some objects. I could move fingers individually on command. My sensation started to improve. I started to differentiate between sharp and soft

edges and different textures. My body was changing. My
nerves were beginning to reignite, and I was healing. My
peers would have killed to have been in my shoes . . .

And, I was grateful.

Others in the hospital were unhappy, and rightfully
so—in fact, I don't think anyone could be happy to have a
spinal cord injury. However, having an injury and feeling
badly about it are two different things. With objective
reasoning, you know you can't change the injury—but, you
can change how you feel. You *can* choose gratitude. It's all
about perspective . . .

It's your choice.

I was thankful I had movement in my fingers, at all, and
that would be my perspective—thankful for what I had, not
fixating on all I lost.

Gratitude's power for all of us lies in its ability to help
us overcome adversity. It helps us frame setbacks in the
grand scheme of things, choosing the perspective of 'things
aren't so bad.' It helps us pick ourselves up when we've been
knocked down. However, it's counterintuitive to activate
gratitude when you're feeling down—it takes effort and
practice.

The sad reality is most people don't get better from a
spinal cord injury—they have to adjust their lives. While I
was making adjustments, I was determined—destined—to
get better—and, I felt it with my heart and soul.

I was making progress, and it was only a matter of time
before things really turned for the better.

Chapter 10

WEEK 5

My legs showing signs of strength and sensation returning, I could barely feel the skin on my thighs, as well as pressure in my toes and the bottoms of my feet. Abdominal muscles started to engage, responding to my cues, and my arm strength was improving. I came a long way from the first time I tried to lift a one-pound dumbbell off the countertop in my room! Then, it felt glued to the counter, and I dropped it on the floor immediately after getting it airborne, my grip-strength practically non-existent.

Since then, I worked hard in the gym with the help of adaptive aids like a wrist strap for the cable gym. My strength returned to a point where I was able to turn myself over at night without the need of nurse support every three hours.

I could almost sit up on my own!

Transferring in and out of bed using the ceiling sling became far too cumbersome, so, I learned—with the help of my physiotherapist—how to support some of my weight with my legs and feet. Using my arms to push, I could swing my butt from my bed to my wheelchair and back—by simply learning to transfer in and out of my wheelchair, it afforded a massive amount of freedom.

That mastered, I put myself to bed, and got up on my own accord. It was so amazing, and I felt an overwhelming wave of gratitude each time I made the transfer. Once I started standing in physio, the feeling only intensified. Every time my feet touched the floor, boom! Gratitude triggered! It didn't matter which side of the bed I got out of—my feet touched the floor, and boom! Gratitude!

Then, an ah-ha moment.

I realized I could harness the feeling. I could purposefully activate gratitude, identifying my own gratitude triggers, to pull me out of depression.

Trust me—if I can do it, you can, too.

It could be your first cup of coffee in the morning if it's something you're sincerely thankful for, or the moment you reach for the door handle on your car before driving to work each morning. Maybe that moment triggers you to feel thankful you have a car, you can get to work, and you're lucky to earn a paycheck.

If you have young kids, maybe it's the moment you wake them up for school in the morning. They bounce out of bed, all bright-eyed and bushy-tailed, ready to take on the school day . . . or, maybe your coffee moment is *before* you wake them up! You can probably tell I'm not a parent . . .

Gratitude gives me perspective. It helped me heal mentally and emotionally, so I could focus on doing the work to heal physically. Like me, it can help you overcome any challenge in your way.

The reason elite athletes—the best in the world—achieve success is because they're exceptional at overcoming adversity. They're better at handling challenges than their competitors, and that's why they win—it's a combination of perspective and persistence. Sure, there's a level of talent and competency involved, but they achieve competency through practice.

Professional athletes set themselves apart from the amateurs by the way they practice. Amateur athletes practice until they get it right—professional athletes practice until they can't get it wrong. Once you get to the top level in any sport, all of your competitors share a level of competence rivaling your own. So, if it's not skill setting you apart, what does?

Your mindset.

It's why the best athletes, business leaders, coaches, and parents have an aptitude for gratitude. Gratitude is a foundational component of their mindsets, and it's an influence tool for leaders. But, its greatest strength is in its ability to help us overcome adversity.

Think about it—how many of you have ever seen a team win a championship, or an athlete win gold when, in post-game or post-competition interviews, they aren't quick to give thanks?

It just doesn't happen.

They thank their coaches, trainers, teammates, and families—their teams. While it seems like an obvious time for someone to be thankful, the tendency to lean toward gratitude is a perspective cultivated over time.

If gratitude is deeply ingrained—intrinsically integrated into your life—it creates incredible results. But, it only becomes the default disposition when we bring awareness to our sense of gratitude, and when gratitude becomes a regular practice.

Tiger Woods won the 2019 Masters Tournament and, in part, it's thanks to gratitude. In his post-championship interview while wearing the infamous green jacket, Tiger said, "I'm very fortunate to have had a procedure to alleviate the pain I was in—now, I'm just stiff." Referring, of course, to his recent lumbar fusion surgery he had in 2017 on his lower back.

"I'm just so thankful," he continued, "to have had the opportunity to play at the elite level again, and . . . um . . . to have won a couple of tournaments. But, to have won a major championship? I'm going to soak this one in a little bit . . ."

Tiger was simply grateful to be playing. He was grateful to be there, physically, and it was possible because of his surgery. He overcame insurmountable odds to win—which, you can argue is the greatest come-back story in sports history. He exemplifies what makes elite athletes and leaders so successful . . .

The ability to overcome great adversity.

Gratitude's power for all of us lies in its ability to help us overcome challenges. It helps us frame setbacks in the grand scheme of things, realizing things could always be worse. It helps us pick ourselves up when we're knocked down.

But, it's counterintuitive to activate gratitude when you're feeling down. It isn't automatic for us to gravitate to gratitude if we're in the valley bottom—for it to become default takes practice.

Do you think Tiger was only grateful when he won the Masters? Of course not—he felt gratitude while on the course, whether or not it were a championship match.

When I was a young skier, I had plenty of injuries holding me back from achieving my potential, skiing the way I wanted to, and competing against my friends. So, when I was healthy, I vividly remember the internal dialogue I used to take stock, appreciating I could ski the way I wanted. I felt thankful for those moments because I knew in freestyle skiing, injury was common. Any day on the mountain could be my last day of the season if I got hurt.

Practicing gratitude—like pro athletes practice their sports—is imperative if you want gratitude to become your default pattern. It's easy to feel thankful when you win—you know, when things are going well. It's natural. However, it's unnatural and counterintuitive to feel thankful when you're feeling low. When things are dark and you're at the valley bottom, you must intentionally practice gratitude until it becomes your default. Only then, will you fall back on it when the going gets tough.

Deep valley bottoms are always accompanied by high mountain peaks. When you're in the valley bottom feeling low, gratitude can help lift you up. Gratitude can help give you the fortitude to take your first step back up the mountain trail.

It's important to realize there's balance in almost everything in life. Those low valley bottoms feel dark because you know what it feels like to stand on top of a mountain peak in the sun. For most of us, we spend the majority of our lives somewhere above the mid-line, pretty high up on the mountain. We venture to the top, but rarely drop all the way down to the depths of the valley floor. That's why, when you find yourself in the depths of hell, it feels so dark. We can't hope to rely on gratitude only when the going gets tough— when the going gets tough, we need to be ready.

Gratitude triggers are a great way to help you practice gratitude every day. Your triggers—something for which you're sincerely thankful—will remind you to take a moment for mindful gratitude.

There are other ways you can practice, too. If you're reading this, it means you're a leader in some capacity. Some people don't consider themselves to be leaders, but I believe all of us are leaders because everyone has influence. If you work with other people and your colleagues listened to one of your ideas, it means you're a leader. All parents are leaders. All athletes are required to take the ball and run with it when the time comes.

As leaders, an obvious way to activate gratitude is to start saying thank you frequently. Give thanks where praise is due—insincere gratitude, though, will backfire. However, if thanks you give is genuine and thoughtful, it will not only motivate the person you're thanking, it will lift your spirits in the process.

So, think about this . . . how can you and your team benefit if gratitude becomes part of your daily best practices?

Well, gratitude serves to reinforce pro-social behavior in coworkers, partners, and teammates. It also influences people with whom you interact outside of your immediate team.

For example, according to the Journal of Marketing in a test of positive reinforcement of customers (1976), one experiment found customers of a jewelry store who were called and thanked, showed a subsequent 70% increase in return purchases. In comparison, customers who were called and told about a sale showed only a 30% increase in purchases, and customers who weren't called at all didn't show an increase.[1]

Have you ever had a server at a restaurant write thank you on your check? Why do they do that? Because, a study from the Journal of Applied Social Psychology found regular patrons of restaurants gave bigger tips when servers wrote, 'Thank you' on their checks.[2]

The feeling of genuine appreciation has significant impact. In the workplace, employee motivation, effort, and commitment have a direct correlation to the sense of gratitude they feel from their employer, manager, company, or organization. It's proven employee motivation and productivity increase when feeling your work is truly appreciated. The result?

People who feel valued, put forward their best efforts.

---

1 Carey, J. R., Clicque, S. H., Leighton, B. A., & Milton, F. (1976). A test of positive reinforcement of customers. Journal of Marketing, 40, 98-100.

2 Rind, B., & Bordia, P. (1995). Effect of server's "Thank you" and personalization on restaurant tipping. Journal of Applied Social Psychology, 25, 745-751.

So, let's activate the power of gratitude! This is a mindfulness exercise, and I need you to use your head and heart.

Visualize and feel as we go through this exercise—first, think about an object or an experience. It can be something you own, or an activity you do. The object or experience is something you love, and you're thankful it's in your life.

Please take a moment to think about it, holding it in your mind's eye and your heart, and feel free to close your eyes if you wish . . .

Okay! How does it feel? It's easy to smile, isn't it? It sort of gives you the warm fuzzies, right?

The second thing—well, it's not actually a thing—is a person, someone in your life whom you love, at the same level or more than the object or experience. The person is someone in your life, who, even though you love them, you could be more grateful for him or her—perhaps, you unintentionally take that person for granted once in a while.

Think about how taking them for granted makes you feel.

Please take a few moments . . .

It doesn't feel as good, does it? You may be feeling uncomfortable—but, why? Well, maybe it's guilt.

Maybe, you might want to take action to let that person know you're thankful they're in your life.

I strongly recommend you do.

That's the power of gratitude.

In a matter of moments, we can feel warm fuzzies, discomfort, or borderline guilt—and, all can make us feel compelled to take action.

Gratitude helps us overcome adversity, but it can also take us far beyond the baseline. In a world struggling with resilience and mental toughness, it can take us from surviving to thriving. And, grateful leaders who understand the power of such a useful tool will have a more profound influence on their followers.

This quote from Francois van Vuuren sums up gratitude relating to motivation . . .

"Gratitude compels you to do your best, not from a basis of performance, but from a basis of true realization of what you have been given in life. These gifts, which you appreciate, should never be taken for granted."

I thinks that's true—grateful people tend to be more proactive when attaining their personal and organizational goals, and are more inclined to help others in need.

The benefits of gratitude are significant. Grateful people live in the moment and recognize others for their efforts frequently. They're more coachable and approachable and, with gratitude, it's easier to recognize the gift of opportunity, and work harder for it.

It helps us look for the silver lining in every situation, and gratitude becomes intrinsically motivating. You'll notice the effects of gratitude on motivation by improved resilience, work ethic, relationships, and productivity.

It certainly accelerated my healing trajectory while at G.F. Strong. Over time, whether I were in physiotherapy, occupational therapy, hand therapy, or just going through the motions of my day, I started to feel more grateful on a regular basis. Times I lost heart or felt despair, depression, and frustration, I turned into opportunities for shifting my perspective to become more objective, to recognize opportunities, and to learn because I was conscious of my ability to feel thankful.

I started to live by the words 'grateful every day.' I even started using the hashtag #gratefuleveryday in all of my communication through Facebook or Instagram with the outside world.

Before I knew it, gratitude became part of my routine, and the foundational strength it gave me helped me take my first steps.

Chapter 11

WEEK 6

I wheeled myself down to the physiotherapy center in the hospital like I did every day. Finally, I graduated to a manual, push wheelchair from the power wheelchair which was helping me build up my arm strength.

As I glided into the gymnasium to find Peter, my 6' 8" giant of a physiotherapist, he greeted me with his usual big smile. But, that day, something was different—I could tell he had something up his sleeve.

"What do you say we get you out of that chair today," he asked casually.

"You mean it? Am I ready?" Pretty sure I was grinning from ear-to-ear!

We were working on my hip mobility and strength by isolating the joint in a kneeling position during our previous sessions, so I knew what was about to happen. I wasn't wearing the best footwear for it—my slippers, albeit comfortable, weren't great walking shoes—but, I wasn't about to let that deter me.

After a few minutes, I was ready to go. Peter put on my harness—much like the jolly jumper setup I had at Vancouver General Hospital—attaching me to the ceiling lift in the physio gym.

Then, it was time.

I sat in my chair, facing a walker, harnessed in and ready to go. "Okay—1-2-3, lift!" Peter held me by the harness to support my movement.

I leaned forward with my torso to get my center of gravity over my feet and, as soon as I felt my body over my base of support, I pushed with everything I had.

"Peter! Did you help?"

"No! That was all you! I have you, though . . ." Peter moved into position to make sure I wouldn't fall. His assistant tightened the ceiling lift just enough so it was a safety precaution, not supporting my weight.

I gripped the walking frame in front of me as tightly as I could. With braces on both knees designed to stop my joints from hyper-extending and bending backwards, I had very little control over my legs. Without feeling what was happening, I looked straight ahead.

"Okay—try to move your right leg toward me," Peter instructed.

With all of my focus and strength, my right foot moved ever so slightly forward. *Holy shit!* Again, with all of my effort, it jumped ahead a few inches. Then left, then right!

I took my first steps!

I made it fourteen feet across the room before collapsing back into my wheelchair, exhausted.

But, I did it.

Well, as you can imagine, I was overwhelmed, gratitude rushing through my body. I just defied all odds! After being told I would never walk again, I proved the experts wrong. I proved to myself I could do it!

Over the coming weeks, I noticed steady improvements, the swelling in my spinal cord decreasing considerably, permitting increased sensory feedback and neuropathic transmission than prior weeks. I went from walking fourteen feet across the physio center with a jolly jumper harness and a walker to walking in the parallel bars, then strolling around the gym with my physiotherapist. Then, finally, I was walking with forearm crutches, navigating the hallways.

I conquered the three-week no-accidents threshold, so I was granted access to the swimming pool. I wasn't swimming laps, but I was walking laps! The support of the water and my body's buoyancy meant I could really start to find my stride.

I advanced to walking to and from the cafeteria at mealtime—there was always a much better selection there than on the ward, and I was thrilled!

But, not everyone was happy for me.

Many of my peers looked on with resentment, which was pivotal for me, and I remember walking into the cafeteria for the first time. It took all of my strength to make it from the third floor, down the elevator, through the line to order food, then make my way to the tables. I approached a group of other hospital inmates—I mean, patients. Sitting around a table were four or five guys in wheelchairs with varying levels of disability.

I ate lunch with them for the previous couple of weeks, and I considered them good guys. We supported each other, rooting for each other in the healing journey—or, so I thought. As I got close, I realized there wasn't a chair for me at the table—not surprisingly, they brought their own.

One of the guys—an abrasive man I estimated to be in his late forties who crashed his jeep end over end—looked up at me. I knew he hated being in a wheelchair. Who wouldn't? But, his perspective was particularly bleak. "Look at you," he commented. "You can't sit here with us no more like that!" Then, he flipped me the bird.

I looked on without saying a word. My mind was in fight or flight—I hadn't been threatened like that previously and, in that moment, I decided to take flight. *Is that so*, I thought. *Fine by me . . .*

"C'mon, man! I was joking!"

I didn't care. I carried on walking across the cafeteria to one of the empty tables that had a regular chair—by then, I needed to collapse.

As difficult as it was, the man in this story did me a favor. In hindsight, he gave me a gift—I knew I couldn't stay there. I couldn't remain in the hospital, surrounded by resentment. Not everyone was healing like I was—in fact, no one was healing like me. I knew my good fortune because I could see the alternative around me at every turn. I was so close to being a complete quadriplegic, but, for some reason, my injury was incomplete. I was getting better. There was no saying how much better I would get, but I knew if I stayed in the rehab center, it wasn't going to do me any favors. I needed to grow. I needed to heal and surround myself with people who would support that vision.

I needed to leave the hospital.

That meant I needed to go back to real life. Besides, for someone who loves being outside, three months is a long time to spend inside.

Especially, inside a hospital.

—Week 13—

I set a goal when I got to G.F. Strong in one of my first meetings with my medical team, and they told me not to expect it to happen. "Don't attach yourself to an outcome," one commented—which is good advice because it's better to focus on the process rather than the product. Of course, the doctors were acting in my best interest—I think. Or, maybe they were protecting their own behinds. Or, maybe they saw enough cases like mine, and they knew it was a long shot.

I packed everything in my room, surprised I accumulated a number of belongings over my three-month stay—I might as well have been packing up a small apartment! As it turned out, a wheelchair doubled as a good trolley, and I used it to wheel all of my stuff out the hospital's front doors!

In just three months—not twelve like I was originally told—I walked out of the hospital, shattering the goal I set for myself just weeks earlier.

It was monumental.

They told me it wouldn't be possible. They told me I wouldn't walk again.

They told me, but I never believed it.

While I took my wheelchair with me, I was free of the confines of the hospital, and chair. I was free!

G.F. Strong, as we used to joke, stands for "Get Fucking Strong," which is exactly what I did. I grew more in the prior three months mentally, emotionally, and physically than I had in the previous ten years. There was no question I was put through an intensive, perspective shifting, fast-track course on the meaning of life. I changed, and the lessons learned couldn't be more valuable because I was just starting my journey. The challenges I was about to face would require every bit of my fortitude, gratitude, mental, and emotional strength to overcome.

I was free.

But, what waited for me in the outside world would test me beyond what I could have ever imagined . . .

Chapter 12

Bouncing Back

I f you're not falling, you're not trying.

That was a huge part of freestyle skiing, and life in general. If you don't fail, you don't learn. A lot of people view failure as a negative—or, when it happens, they have a hard time picking themselves up. Why? Because they might not correlate it with progress, or they might not have that type of mentality.

So, there I was, gripping the car's 'holy-shit' handle, riding shotgun in a black four-door sedan adorned with a roof rack and ski gear. We precariously navigated our way through the snowy mountain pass, Revelstoke our final destination and home to Revelstoke Mountain Resort, boasting the most vertical skiing terrain in North America at

5620 feet. A mountain so large, if you don't pay it the respect it's due, it can swallow you whole. Not kidding—people have lost their lives navigating its vast terrain.

Seems like the perfect place for me to take my first crack at skiing again, right?

I was out of the hospital for two weeks and, during a meeting with my surgical specialist in Vancouver before the trip, I was cleared to go skiing only three-and-a-half months after my accident.

Okay—'cleared' isn't quite accurate. "Mike," my surgeon said, "as long as you don't do anything that jars your neck in under four months from your initial surgery, you should be fine. The titanium in your neck is still fusing and becoming part of your body as the bone grows around it . . ."

So, I went home and told my mom I was cleared to go sit-skiing by my doctor! As an aside, I owe Mom a fortune for hair dye over the years—I may not be the entire reason she went gray, but pretty close.

At the time, skiing on my own two feet was out of the question, but, with the help of the Live It Love It Foundation, I could return to the mountains during the same winter as my injury in a sit-ski! Live It Love It supports people who sustained spinal cord injuries, and they were helping me like they helped others get back to living a full life—the life I wanted to live. With the help of an adaptive sit-ski—basically a fiberglass chair mounted to a pair of skis—I could accomplish my next goal of getting back to the mountains.

What better place to learn to sit-ski than Revelstoke?

With adrenaline flooding my veins before we even got to the ski hill, I was exhilarated with the thought of an adventure with friends, including Darren Rayner and Jan Schuster, both responsible for the filming. Cinematographers by trade, they operate a production company in Vancouver, BC, and were taking turns filming my recovery. In the early days, we didn't know what we'd do with the footage, especially while I was in the hospital. But, I was making such incredible progress with my healing, we continued to document the journey. Making my first turns in a sit-ski would definitely be an event worth capturing on film!

After parking in VIP spots at the resort—what I called handicap parking stalls—we met up with the Live It Love It crew including Jeff, its founder. He greeted us with a smile and a radiating sense of stoke, his energy embodying the fun we were going to have on the mountain that day. Jeff is a quadriplegic with limited arm function, and not much in the way of hand function—but, what he lacks in physical ability, he makes up for in tenacity and vision. His mission is to get back to empower through adventure, and bring as many people as possible along for the ride. He selected me for the Live It Love It 'Make Their Day' event, and I couldn't have been more stoked to be there!

Jeff and I were fitted into our sit-skis with the help of the Revelstoke Adaptive Sports Program volunteers and, soon, we were loading into the gondola, ascending the 5620-foot behemoth. Not gonna lie—I had butterflies which were refreshingly familiar. I lived for that feeling frequently in my past life on skis, and nerves provided great comfort.

When I was young, I used to think nerves were a bad thing—but, I had to listen to my gut feeling, and adjust course. Usually, nerves were there to keep me on edge, and that's a good thing. They were a sort of primer for the nervous system to ready my body and mind for my next move.

In freestyle skiing, I lived for that feeling. If I didn't have butterflies, it meant I wasn't pushing my limits, skiing at my edge. I needed those butterflies and, if I didn't have them, it was hard to get in the zone to ski my best. All the nervous energy welling up inside me before dropping into a skiing contest was potential energy waiting to become kinetic. Once I pushed out the gate, I transferred all of my potential into action.

Think about it—without nerves, there's no reward. It's when we reach the end of a run or cross the finish line we get to appreciate the reward. All the nerves we had at the beginning wash through us in a rush of adrenaline. The oxytocin, dopamine, serotonin, norepinephrine, anandamide, and endorphins—the most addicting neurochemicals—hit us, and it feels incredible!

Plenty of people don't understand extreme sports or how someone could actually enjoy public speaking—but, if we understand what's happening in our bodies when we become nervous, it helps us release ourselves from fear. We take risks we potentially might not otherwise.

So, there we were—in the gondola, our conversation light-hearted and fun. I kept asking questions about how it was going to go—in the back of my mind, I knew the risk. I couldn't jar my neck, risking damage to the titanium rods.

It wasn't an option.

I said to my sit-skiing instructor, "Whatever happens today, we need to take it easy. I don't want to go too far out of my comfort zone . . ."

"Absolutely—that's not the name of the game today," He paused, focusing on me. "It's to get out on the hill, have fun, get fresh air. The crew is stoked!"

"Great, how about this? If things get too gnarly, let's have a safety word. If I scream WHISKEY, it means we need to dial it back—okay?"

"Check! Today is going to be a fun day . . ."

Finally, we unloaded at the top of the gondola, got situated in our sit-skis, and we were off! As soon as I started to glide down the hill, I felt it—my nerves turned kinetic, and I hadn't felt more alive over the last three-and-a-half months. There were about eight people with us, all feeling the good vibes, hooting and hollering as wind and frigid air grazed our cheeks as we picked up speed.

Starting on the easiest slope, I traversed back and forth down the hill, getting the hang of things, leaning left and right, extending each arm using my outriggers as they were intended. In each hand, I held a short metal pole looking like fore-arm crutches with small, foot-long plastic skis on each end—the outriggers helped balance and turn the skis when I leaned.

My ski instructor was happy with the progress I was making throughout the day. We started out with his skiing behind me, holding on to the back of my chair and, as time passed, he gained confidence and let go. I was free! He did keep a bit of a tight leash on me, tethered to the sit-ski, so I was never completely out of reach.

His help was comforting.

I couldn't believe it! I was skiing again! The same winter I broke my neck! It was my goal to go back the mountains, but I had no idea it could happen so soon. I wasn't skiing the way I used to, but I learned to do it in a different way. The opportunity to sit-ski shifted my perspective dramatically after the first few turns. I knew if I never skied again on my own two feet, I could still be back on the hill with friends, taking in views, breathing mountain air, living and loving the adrenaline. It was then I truly realized my life had so much meaning.

Before the last run of the day, everyone was feeling elated and exhausted—especially me, and I made sure to let my instructor and crew know I was feeling bagged. Everyone set off down the mountain, destined for the lodge, and the run was going so well, they were jumping around, playfully taking full advantage of the soft snow. I hit a soft pillow-like mound which erupted in front of me, dousing my face with frozen crystals, adding to the glorious feeling of being alive.

We arrived at a gathering point at a trail junction, three quarters of the way down the mountain. To our right, the easy way down via a wide winding track traversing the mountain back and forth. To the left, a steep, double fall-line pitch with a large embankment off the left side.

"Which way do we go," I asked.

"To the left," Jeff informed us, "is snow-rodeo. It's a bit more challenging, but a much shorter way to get back to the lodge. To the right, we take the cat-track . . ."

I looked out at the ski run, assessing the options.

"I think you've got Snow-Rodeo . . ."

As soon as the words left his mouth some of the others in the group took off down the hill, and we followed suit. I started linking turns just as I'd been doing, but navigating the pitch was a challenge. The double fall-line meant it wasn't a wide open run, facing one direction. The contour of the slope funneled toward the embankment on the left side, narrowing toward the bottom.

I started picking up speed, heading toward the bank. I knew I had 'Whiskey' in my back pocket, but I chose not to use it.

I knew I could make the next turn.

Bearing quickly to the left across the run with no easy way to slow down, approaching the bank, I gave it my all—and, in one deep turn away from the bank, I felt a tug on the tethers, and the ski instructor behind me yelled. Then, in a moment of chaos, the sled turned back toward the steep bank, then back again—a speed wobble from hell. BAM! I caught the down-hill edge of the ski, perpendicular to the inclination of the ski run, high-siding, and started to tumble.

In a sit-ski, when flipping end over end, there's only really one part of the body making contact with the snow. I felt my head pummel the snow and kick back so violently, when the ski went over the top of me, the hefty plastic buckle on the seat belt fastening me to the chair, snapped.

My limp body flew out of the chair.

When the dust settled, there I was, lying on the snow, breathing in a panic. I couldn't move. "Oh, my God! Oh, my God! I want to get out! I want to get out!"

I tried again. Maybe my body was stunned the first time, I don't know, but I wiggled my toes on the second attempt, relief washing over me. *Am I stupid!? Why did I ever come out here? Why did I think sit-skiing was a good idea? This was exactly what WASN'T supposed to happen!*

"My neck! Ouch! My neck!" My friends rushed to my side in a familiar scene, and I was taken back to the moment when I crashed just a few months earlier, shuddering at the thought I could have broken my neck again.

"Mike! Mike! Are you okay? Tell us you're okay!" Darren was standing over me, camera rolling.

"I think I'm good, but that wasn't part of the plan! My head kicked back . . ." It sickened me considering the fact I could have had another catastrophic injury resulting from the crash.

In reflection, the whole sit-skiing experience was a big eye-opener. I had to pick myself up and keep going, but I needed to spend some time working on my body. I had a long way to go if I ever wanted to ski again upright—and, the biggest eye-opener was I needed to take it in stride. I couldn't let the crash keep me down.

I needed to remain resilient.

Chapter 13

EXPLORING RESILIENCE

I n the previous chapter, we explored gratitude's being a key component of resilience. The reason elite athletes—like great leaders, entrepreneurs, or parents—achieve success is because they're incredibly exceptional at overcoming adversity. Gratitude is a foundational, cornerstone value for the most successful people on the planet, and it's important because of the perspective shift accompanying a 'gratitude attitude.' It helps us frame setbacks in the grand scheme of things and, when we think about all we have to be thankful for, it gives us a mental and emotional boost. It propels us to take the next step forward, helping us become more resilient.

Resilience in today's world is a critical attribute defining whether people make the transition from surviving to thriving. In life, there will be doldrums, but don't lose heart—don't lose faith, and believe you have the ability to succeed. Obstacles in your way—side steps, or steps backward—

are opportunities for growth. With that in mind, you can develop your ability to be more resilient, take adversities in stride, and achieve your goals.

Some people believe you're either resilient, or you're not. Many people can handle hard times, others can't. Some thrive. Some dive. But, here's the thing—everyone is resilient, and we have been since the time we were born. Why? Because humans are survivors—from the moment we enter this world, our bodies and minds are working to survive. If we're sick, our bodies work to heal us. If we're threatened, we do whatever's necessary to fight back—but, as we grow and age, there's a depth of resilience surging beyond mere survival instincts.

It's true—we'll pick ourselves up when we're knocked down. It doesn't matter if you fall on the ski hill or in the grocery store—you'll pick yourself up.

What changes as we go through life isn't the question of whether or not we're resilient—it's the challenges we face. Our adversities never remain constant, but we continuously face hardship in some form, and those hardships are different for everyone. What's hard for me, might not be hard for you—and, vice versa. You get the idea . . .

It's about humility.

You never know what someone is going through, or what they might find impossible until you walk a mile in their shoes. A cliché, I know—but, it's the truth.

Not everyone goes through a disabling injury, but all lose loved ones—grief happens. However, in life, most challenges we face have varying levels of difficulty. No matter the issue, the skill sets we possess will dictate how hard we perceive a problem to be—if we have the tools to do the job and the solution is readily available, then the problem isn't much of a problem, at all. Resilience is one of the tools in our tool kits for any challenge.

I mentioned resilience is innate in all of us—the difference between people who are resilient and those who aren't is practice. Our collective experiences in life—managing adversity and facing challenges while learning to overcome obstacles—dictate the level of resilience you possess. Of course, that's fantastic news for all of us! If it changes over time, it means we can work on it and improve. We can become more resilient, and it starts with how we approach a problem.

When we have a challenging conversation, do we stand tall, or do we crumble? When we feel threatened by another person who's questioning us and our ideas when trying to solve a problem, do we remain objective and rational? Or, do we become emotional and scattered? When the problem seems so big, and there's no solution in sight, do we give up? Or, do we change our strategy?

Can we stay committed to our mission?

I know—it's tough. But, during times we're tested, we have to remain objective and rational. In the beginning, there will be times we won't have tools in our kits to solve a problem—however, with solution-based thinking and a broader perspective, it's possible to find a way. The truth is trying to sidestep or circumventing an obstacle rarely works, and hardship or adversity in our way become *the way*. In life, things holding us back—problems—are the solutions. If we find ways to surpass limiting adversities, it primes us for success because, in the process, things we learn cultivate skills, traits, and attributes making us successful in the long run.

Resilience is the tool in everyone's tool kit helping us overcome our challenges. So, with your next challenge or the problem you're facing right now, try to remain objective. Choose a perspective of gratitude for the tools you currently have in your arsenal helping you to thrive. Search for new strategies when it seems there are none available. Source alternate skill sets. Approach your problem with rational reasoning and, above all, know you have it within yourself to push through . . .

You are resilient.

Your ability to succeed lies in beliefs you have about yourself. If you believe you're resilient and you have what it takes, you're going to succeed. Your beliefs influence emotions, and how you feel about a situation. They, in turn, influence your thoughts and rationale with which you approach tough situations. Your thoughts influence behavior, and actions you choose will make the difference in whether you go from surviving to thriving.

That day on the mountain at Revelstoke almost ended in disaster. I was offered a snowmobile ride down the mountain at that point, but I opted out. I decided I would sit-ski the rest of the way down to the lodge, an action taking more mental fortitude than physical. Not only that, I decided to go the following day because I knew if I didn't get back in the saddle, I might never get back in a sit-ski. With so many unknowns for my future recovery, I had to keep the door open.

It's funny—I recall that particular crash with more PTSD than the one when I broke my neck. The saving grace in that whole scenario was I tried again, not admitting defeat, when I could have taken the easy road.

I'm glad I got back on the horse, and skied the rest of the way down.

—Month 5—

Going back to real life wasn't easy.

While I walked out of the hospital and pretty much straight into a sit-ski, I still couldn't handle being on my feet for more than a few minutes at a time. Fortunately, I had my wheelchair to fall back on, but I worked as hard as I could to stand for longer periods.

I heard when people leave G.F. Strong, it can be a big shock—and, it's true. I went from having twenty-four seven nurse support to having to take care of all of my personal care routines. I had to cook for myself a lot of the time, and I had to take responsibility for my life. Another truth?

I struggled with my disability.

Some days, simply going to the grocery store took everything I had, and there were times I felt as if I weren't getting better. *What if I stay like this? What if I need to rely on a wheelchair my whole life?*

Thoughts I didn't like . . .

Those were the times my mind went to pessimistic places—which, I think, is normal. All of us have the angel and devil on our shoulders—which voice we choose to listen to is up to us. Me? I kept coming back to gratitude, using it as fuel on the fire to remain resilient.

The sit-ski crash was an eye opener, and I needed to keep working hard at my recovery, especially if I wanted to ski again. I had to accept responsibility for my situation, realizing if I wanted to get out of it and improve the state of my life—well, that was on me, and no one could do the work for me. I needed to start taking steps forward, even if they were baby steps.

I needed forward momentum.

My path to that point in my life hadn't been without setbacks, especially in the hospital, or on the ski hill in Revelstoke. I knew I was destined to fail at times. I just needed to take things one step at a time—a valuable lesson for all of us. No matter the challenges we face, take responsibility, and move on.

All of us fail from time to time—there's no doubt about it. The question is how do we fail forward? How do we turn our failure into a learning opportunity? We don't grow from easy things in life—we grow from the difficult things. We know what happens when we work easy—we reap minimal rewards. What happens if we work easy instead of working hard? Do we grow? Of course not—we need to work hard to see results. What happens when we do?

We level up in the world.

Skills and abilities it took you to get to this point in your life aren't the same skills taking you to your next level. For progress, you need to learn, adapt, and grow. Failure is, after all, the mechanism for learning. It's part of the progress process—without it, you won't level up. With that in mind, it's much easier to release yourself from the fear of failure. It's no longer something you'll avoid . . .

It's something you'll embrace.

In the summer of 2014—after I moved home with my mom and stepdad and settled into a rehab routine of physiotherapy and strength training five days a week—I stayed laser focused on a goal I had since the moment I woke up from surgery and was told I'd never walk again.

I needed to get back on skis.

My training and rehabilitation took on new meaning with skiing in mind—it always did—but, that was different. I trained myself and my athletes in the gym before my accident—not to get buff, but so we could ski harder. Working out achieved logic-supported injury prevention—if I were strong enough to take big slams and pick myself up to keep skiing, it was a good thing. On top of that, tricks got easier with every bit of newly gained strength.

For me, it wasn't a matter of taking big crashes and picking myself up—I did that enough while freestyle skiing, and in the sit-ski. The question was whether or not I could do it—period. I didn't know. At five months out from my accident, I was still walking on forearm crutches, unable to manage walking more than a few hundred meters at a time. My body was the paltry shadow of its athletic self . . .

My first workout? In my parents' basement. I stood in front of the mirror in my underwear, disgraced by my reflection. I weighed about 150 pounds and, at 6'2", I was a bone rack, not weighing so little since I was fourteen years old. I had my work cut out for me, but, fortunately, I didn't have anything else to do but treat my recovery like my day job—and, I chose to work overtime.

I looked at my bony frame like a blank slate and, if I were an artist, my muscular system was my canvas. With the help of my physiotherapists, I started from scratch, building my body from the inside out, beginning with minute stabilizer muscles between the vertebral joints and ribs. At first, my pelvic floor and transverse abdominals took a bit of coaxing to start firing—once they did, I used elastic physio bands, my body weight, a bosu ball, and a standard exercise ball to strengthen my core. My weight training routine involved five-to-ten pound dumbbells, a grind, mentally and physically. Much like in the hospital, I had to preemptively dose myself with pain killers to make it through my workouts.

I was still on oxycodone, months after the accident. I needed them—I mean, *really* needed them. One of the not-so-fun struggles I was dealing with was a physical dependency and addiction to the pain pill. Opioids are brutal, and I didn't understand until I was dependent, it was out of my control. I couldn't just stop taking them cold-turkey. Trust me, I tried. It was horrible—I couldn't sleep, my skin was on fire and unbearably itchy, and I was angry without the drug. I wasn't myself. My body lashed out at me with headaches and temperature swings, and I felt hot and cold. I needed my oxy even though I didn't want it because it made me lethargic, a space cadet, and it slurred my speech.

Brutal.

Unwanted as they were, the opioids were a comfort, numbing everything, including my mind. They were a detrimental way to escape my emotional pain as much as the physical. My recovery may have sped up slightly from my ability to push through painful physical plateaus—but, with every dose, I was putting off my mental and emotional healing. It numbed *everything*. To this day, I know the mental and emotional pain I endured through the early months were worse than the physical.

So, I made a plan with my doctor to slowly lower my dose, weaning me off the horrible stuff—I needed to find a balance. I realized I couldn't push too hard in therapy, otherwise the pain was too much, and it made me want the pain-relieving warmth of the oxycodone. I got really good at listening to my body, pumping the brakes when I needed to give myself a break. In fact, I never was good at that—I lived my life almost entirely with my foot on the gas pedal, rarely giving myself a break, going hard until I crashed. It was almost an inevitability something would have to give—I just didn't think it would be my neck.

I had plenty of chances for wakeup calls in my life— suspensions in school, car accidents, broken bones, near death experiences, and people telling me I needed to slow down. I could have listened. I should have listened. I know now paying attention to warning signs in life is a good idea.

As you can imagine, I didn't listen to the wakeup calls until I had a complete awakening. Following my accident, I took a deeper dive into unfamiliar, dark places of my soul—places new to me. My mental and emotional capacity expanded immensely, and I felt awake—I had balance for the first time in my life. I was listening to my body, my inner voice, and spirit more than I ever had, and I felt grounded and connected.

That was my awakening.

But, trust me, you don't want to have to go through trauma to open your mind to see or hear things in a different way—to find balance. All of us can do the work to get in touch with our inner compass to point us in the right direction.

Anyone can find balance.

I found it between working hard physically, working on my mental and emotional capacity, and working to get off the pain pills. Without listening to my body, I couldn't have done it. I was off the pain medication in seven months and that's when my body started to ramp up.

In the first few months after I left the hospital, I built my base, creating a foundation from which to work. My masterpiece—my canvas—was starting to take shape. I put on more weight, and I started walking longer distances, using my walking aids as little as possible. I even learned to ride a bike again! It was just like riding a bike—I didn't forget how, and finding my balance was only a bit of a learning curve.

I worked tirelessly every day to get my body back because I wanted to prove to myself—and, to the world—I could do it. I could beat my spinal cord injury. I could do the impossible by bouncing back from being paralyzed. I knew I was lucky to be healing, at all, so I chose to stay disciplined and motivated.

When I remembered others with injuries in the hospital, even my friends at the table who flipped me the bird in the cafeteria that day, I knew I had to work as hard as I could—if not for myself, for them. I had to work for all the people who would kill to have the same chance to heal.

My ultimate motivation, however?

Skiing.

As winter approached, I took my training seriously—I didn't feel ready, but an important day was approaching. I had my sights set on getting back on snow, and I knew exactly when it was going to happen.

Chapter 14

1 YEAR FROM THE ACCIDENT

—December 16, 2014—

At the base of Whistler mountain, simply putting on my boots was a struggle. My legs were spastic as soon as I entombed my feet in the plastic shells, tightening each buckle one by one. I couldn't tell how tight they were—I still couldn't feel my skin from my waist down. All the effort, the hundreds of hours of physiotherapy and exercises came down to that day.

I was going skiing.

I walked across the parking lot in the Whistler Village to the bottom of the gondola, and I needed my poles for stability. I don't know if it were nervous energy running wild in my body, but my legs weren't cooperating—imagine hooking up electrodes to your legs, turning the meter way up, and having rapid fire electric pulsations shooting through your muscles.

Not fun.

Even so, I pushed it out of my mind. "I'll be fine when I make it to the top," I reassured my friends who were accompanying me.

It was a pretty incredible surprise when I stepped off the gondola—close to fifty people were waiting for me! When I walked out the building doors, I was overwhelmed by cheers, hugs, and laughter. I was incredibly fortunate to have my community supporting me all the way through my journey with SCI, but that moment?

Man . . . I don't have words.

Someone carried my skis to the edge of the ski run, placing them down on the snow. Cautiously, I stepped into the bindings—they felt familiar, but foreign at the same time. The connection with my skis wasn't what it used to be—I couldn't feel my feet—but, I could feel the glide of the skis on the snow as I shuffled them back and forth. "Okay! The moment of truth! I hope this works!" I shouted to the group, as I took off!

Nosing my skis down the fall line of the gentle slope, I started gaining momentum. *Turn!* I sent the message to my legs and, luckily, they were listening. I made my first turn, hearing the roar from my friends behind me. Then, the next turn. And, the next . . .

"I'm doing it! I'm skiing again!" I couldn't contain myself!

I heard a familiar, "Yay, Mikey!" Myles, one of my closest friends and someone who had more influence on my life than most, cheered for me. He was my ski coach for years and my team manager for Atomic and Oakley, as well as a phenomenal skier.

I pulled off to a part of the run where I could stop to catch my breath. Myles skied up and with a massive high five said, "That's one of the coolest things I've ever seen! This is one of the coolest things I've ever been a part of . . ."

"But I didn't even do a trick!" We laughed, knowing it was one of the coolest things I'd done, too. The mountains symbolize adventure, excitement, and adrenaline, and it was amazing to be back out there with my friends. But, it wasn't over yet . . .

I still had to get down the mountain.

I set off again, making my way down the easiest run. The spasticity in my legs hadn't gone away, but I was so filled with joy, I kept going. But, as the run wound down the mountain, I found myself standing at the top of one of the steepest blue runs on Whistler. It's like a bowling alley—a straight shot down one of the steep pitches at mid-mountain.

"Oh, shit! Who chose this run?"

"You did! We're following you," Myles informed me.

He was right. I took a wrong turn. "Well, we better keep going . . ."

I cautiously made my first turn on the steep section, and ice underfoot made it tough to hold a ski edge on the slope. I struggled with the next turn, my legs starting to shake unpleasantly.

"I don't know if I can do this. Why did I take the wrong turn?"

"You got this—just take it one turn at a time." Myles's words took me out of the moment for a brief flash.

"You're right! I've got this . . ."

I could do it—just like I did in physio and workouts, preparing for that moment. The only thing I needed was objectivity—just because I was standing at the top of a steep section wasn't enough reason to get flustered, or deterred. I took a wrong turn—so what? It happened, and there wasn't much I could do about it. Standing at the top of the run was one thing—feeling badly about it was another.

I changed how I felt in a matter of seconds when Myles said, "You've got this . . ."

I started again—and, that's what it took. A start. One turn at a time—baby steps—the whole way down the steep section. When it leveled out at the bottom, my confidence soared! I got through the most difficult part, making it to the green slope. Yes, the slope scaring me only minutes before, seemed far less daunting.

I skied to the bottom of the mountain straight to the Longhorn Saloon. One run was enough, and I needed to rest my exhausted legs!

With a group of close to twenty friends sitting around a long table, I raised my glass, thanking them for being there, picking me up, and supporting me the whole way, not just on that day.

I was grateful for each of them.

I couldn't believe it—I defied the odds! I skied—and, survived to tell the story. I poured all of my effort into achieving that moment, celebrating my return to the mountains as an 'upright.' It was incredible, but, in days following, it left me with a feeling of emptiness . . .

What now?

Chapter 15

FAIL FORWARD

Year 2, Day 1

—December 17, 2014 –

I worked practically non-stop for a year to get back to the mountains, celebrating my monumental achievement with friends in Whistler—but, it was short-lived. While I felt extraordinary gratification from being back in the mountains, I wasn't back skiing the way I used to—far from it. In fact, I only did one run, and had to billy-goat my way down a blue run! I took the easiest way down—and, let's be clear . . . it was only by mistake I took a blue run. In my past life? Triple black diamonds used to be no problem—even fun!

I still had work to do.

But, if it weren't skiing—I checked that one off the list already—what could I work toward? I mean, I needed to keep getting stronger, so I could ski again, but . . . what now?

I heard about an event that could fill my need for challenge and adventure. There was a run taking place in May of 2015 called the Wings for Life World Run. It was a race, and entrants had to run until they couldn't, anymore. Sounds fun, right? Run until you drop?

Not exactly.

There was a way to finish, but the whole premise of the race was 'running for those who can't.' The event was a charity for Spinal Cord Injury, and I knew it was a cause I could champion! I set my sights on the Wings for Life World Run, deciding I was going to participate in Niagara Falls, ON, in May, 2015.

Perfect! I had a new goal to keep me motivated day after day!

I didn't know it at the time, but I was setting myself up for failure—in more ways than one—but, it turned into one of the greatest learning opportunities to fail forward. Beyond learning to walk and ski, I wanted to learn to run again. I wanted to regain my athletic abilities as much as I wanted anything in my life, and the Wings for Life World Run would keep me accountable. It would be a big step in the right direction for physical recovery if I could focus on tackling the race during rehab and physio.

At my physiotherapy center, I was hooked up to a machine—an anti-gravity treadmill, its premise to learn to run or rehabilitate a hip, knee, or ankle without full weight of the body stressing bones, muscles, ligaments, and tendons.

It was fashion-forward—a nice pair of neoprene shorts with a rubber tutu attached around the waist. The tutu zipped into the frame, and an air chamber inflated underneath me to carry up to seventy percent of my body weight.

It was like running on the moon.

After a while, I took my training from the anti-gravity treadmill to a normal treadmill, then onto the ground in an effort to get ready for the Wings for Life World Run which, in itself, was a cool concept. There's a start line, but there's no traditional finish line, the premise being to see how far runners can go, pushing their limits—and, it was for a good cause.

Finding a cure for spinal cord injury.

The best part? One hundred percent of the entry fees go directly to research helping find a cure for spinal cord injuries. And, you know what's really cool? It's a world run with thousands of participants around the globe from the Americas to Oceania, and Europe to Africa. Runners race simultaneously against people from around the world.

Instead of a finish line, a catcher car leaves the start line, tailing runners thirty minutes after the race begins, gradually increasing its pace. Once it catches you, it records your distance using a GPS transmitter—then, you're done.

So, I would be running against the world and myself—while being chased!

Before the race in the spring of 2015, I had to set a goal on the event's website. Naturally, mine was a lofty, but realistic distance—5 miles, or 8 kilometers. Then I clicked the send button, letting everyone in the Facebook universe know my intentions. After all, five miles would be a challenge—but, no big deal because, at that point, I was running over three miles on the treadmill consistently.

However, if you've ever run on a treadmill, you know it's significantly different from running on the ground. The treadmill is repetitive like a hamster wheel, but the ground is full of twists, turns, and elevation changes—and, that means working much harder.

A week before the big race—for which I prepared and trained for the previous four months—I set off to do my first off-the-treadmill run. I made it about a mile from my house when things started to go horribly wrong. My body lit up with pain, my legs spasmed, and I started to limp badly—all the way home. Once I got in the door, I pulled off my shoes and peeled off my socks only to find huge, golf ball sized, blisters on both feet.

Disaster.

Why did I set a goal of 5 miles? I'll never make it! My feet were in so much pain, my back ached, and I had sharp, shooting pains in my neck. Even so, tickets were booked to fly to Niagara Falls, so I knew I had to try.

So, at six forty-five in the morning on May 2, 2015, I lined up with over 700 other Canadians who were supporting the charity by running the race. Precisely at seven, we heard the crack of the starter pistol, and we were off!

I preemptively dosed myself up with pain killers and taped over the blisters on my feet with duct tape before the race, which helped—but, my confidence was still at an all-time low. I knew what was going to happen, and I was right. Just over a mile into the race, my body started to light up with pain.

I don't know which was worse—the physical pain, or realizing I wasn't going to make my goal. I wasn't even close—the race had only started, and I felt done.

At about 1.5 miles into the race, I made it to the part of the course parallel to Niagara Falls. It was a beautiful day—the sun rose moments before the race began, so, by the time I made it to the waterfall, it was golden hour. A mist floated through the air, settling on the road ahead, and I could see rainbows come and go as the sunlight illuminated its color spectrum. When I made it to the section on the road where the mist dampened the asphalt, I brought my awareness to my feet—they were getting more painful as I dragged them along.

Now, I don't know if it were the water on the pavement triggering me, but I suddenly turned my attention to where it needed to be. I thought about how I was running, and the fact I was dragging my toes along the ground with every step, no doubt making my blisters worse.

I knew I couldn't keep going.

I had two options—quit, or try something different. I needed to change my strategy.

Up to that point in my recovery, I worked relentlessly with my physiotherapist to improve my walking gait, strengthening my legs to a point I could run by working on dorsiflexion. I had what's called toe-drop—a hard time engaging muscles in my lower leg and foot to pull my toes upward, toward my knees. I kept focusing on it with every step, but it wasn't working.

On to Plan B.

I wondered what would happen if I pushed. What would happen if I put more effort into pushing down with my toes, working on my plantar flexion by squeezing my calf muscle on every step instead of pulling my toes?

Instead of saying to myself over and over in my mind, *Pull, pull, pull* with every step, I changed to *push, push, push*—and, guess what? I stopped dragging my toes!

By pushing down and raising up on the ball of my foot, it created an extra one-to-two inches of elevation for my opposite leg to swing through, forward, like a pendulum. I wasn't dragging my toes! I couldn't believe it. All I had to do was push instead of pull!

That minor but monumental change in strategy changed the entire outcome of my race that day. I went from thinking I had to quit in a move of self-preservation to running all the way to the 6 mile race marker—10 kilometers—completely obliterating the five-mile goal I set for myself.

It was amazing!

So, how is that failing forward?

Well, I showed up on race day, and stood at the start line with nothing but the thought of failure haunting my mind. There was no way I was going to make it five miles in the race. The result? I failed before I started.

But, I had to try.

About one mile into the race—just like the week prior— my body lit up with pain, and I wasn't going to make it. But, something miraculous happened in those first few miles—I learned more in that small widow of time than I learned in the previous few months of physiotherapy.

I learned the value of failure, and I learned to fail forward.

Now, let's be clear—when we talk about failure, I'm not saying anyone should fail often, fail excessively, or fail for the sake of failing. We must fail mindfully. We must be aware of the impact and consequences of our failures, especially in our businesses, families, and communities. When there are people who rely on us, or whose success depends on ours, sometimes failure isn't an option. However, if we do fail, we can analyze the failure, learn lessons, and adjust our strategies to succeed next time.

It's much better to learn from a small mistake or a close call, rather than having to learn the hard and painful way from a costly mistake. For instance, if you almost miss a deadline for a project you're working on, why did it happen? What caused the near miss? Was it something to do with your routines, or habits needing improvement? Was it a problem within a working-relationship requiring more consistent communication?

Maybe it comes down to a lack of resources.

Questions like those can unveil the root of the problem causing the mistake in the first place. Digging a bit deeper into why the failure happened offers us the ability to prevent it from being repeated.

Most times, when people fail and it's not a significant mistake, we rarely give it a second thought. Yet, we can learn from our mistakes without the message getting lost in the business of our lives. Often, we recognize the mistake, but we move on to the next project or task without proper reflection. It's important the lessons land—we need to acknowledge the 'why,' taking our new information forward so we can try a different strategy. We adapt.

Doing so yields traction. It might not work the first time around and, yes, you might fail again—but, that's just an indication the strategy needs more work. You might have to go back to step one, asking a few more analytical questions, but you absolutely need to keep strategizing, taking the next move.

In the Wings for Life World Run, I enacted the Analyze, Learn, and Change framework. When you face your next failure or close call, ask yourself these critical questions:

—Analyze the Failure: *What happened, and why did things go wrong?*

—Learn the Lessons: *What am I supposed to take away from this?*

—Change the Strategy: *What can I do differently next time?*

Analyzing the failure is the obvious first step. So often when we fail, we let the opportunity for growth pass us by. Lessons go unnoticed because we don't take the opportunity to reflect.

Learning lessons can be challenging at times, especially if the consequence of the failure is significant. But, we need to take in information after our initial analysis, translating it into a takeaway we can use. Once we understand lessons we were meant to learn, we need to change our strategy! What are we going to do now—and, next time—to ensure the failure doesn't happen again, so we'll succeed?

In the 2016 Wings for Life World Run, I changed my strategy. I did multiple 6-mile runs in practice leading up to the event, and I didn't go in ill-prepared like the year before with blisters all over my feet. I increased my capacity, so I could handle long distances, knowing on race day, I'd set a lofty goal of 7.5 miles—or, 12 kilometers. In my head, I was thinking more like 9 or 10 miles.

On race day, I showed up on the start line feeling rested, and ready. I set off, finding my pace early on because I trained at a pace I could sustain for hours, if necessary—which is a good strategy for distance running, but not in the case of Wings for Life. Remember—I was being chased! I needed to go fast! I approached the 6-mile mark in the race after an hour and fifteen minutes, and I felt as if I had a lot of energy left—but, after doing a little quick math in my head, I knew the catcher car wouldn't be far behind. I was going as fast as I could, but my legs just didn't have it in them. I beat my distance from the year before by only a half mile, finishing at 6.5 miles.

I fell far short of my goal! Granted, people were praising the distance, and it was farther than last year—but, in my mind, it was a massive failure!

I didn't make the goal in 2017, only running 4.3 miles while nursing an injury—chalk that one up as a win for self-preservation. My knee was injured due to imbalances in my body, so I had to listen to it, dialing things back.

By 2018, I was feeling ready to take on the goal again. Only that time, I learned lessons from years past, and my strategy changed completely. As soon as the starter's gun went off, I ran as hard as I could for as long as I could to get as far away from the catcher car as possible. A big head start in the Wings for Life World Run has more to do with how far I could go than setting a steady pace I could maintain. I ran as fast as I could until my form started to break. Once I got sloppy and started to notice myself tripping over my own feet, I slowed things down, setting a pace I could maintain for the long run, and the catcher car didn't get me for almost 8 miles!

Failing forward requires us to fail mindfully, sometimes asking ourselves difficult questions. We don't usually like addressing our shortcomings or downfalls, but we need to do the rudimentary analysis so we can identify potential lessons, take them in, and change our approach.

One way to ensure we won't ever grow through failure is to look at it as a bad thing. Instead, we need to look for the flip side—the positive, and how we can grow. Asking tough questions and leaning into and pushing through discomfort, shifts the way we think, as well as how we identify chinks in the armor of the challenge ahead. Such a shift helps us recognize skill gaps we might have, as well as where we need to take steps to improve our game so we can succeed on our next attempt.

Shifting your perspective and turning failure into forward momentum is part of the progress process. With such a mindset, failure becomes the indication of progress. Failure becomes the opportunity for growth, leveling up, and achieving our goals. Remember, though—the intention isn't to fail often or excessively—it's to learn, adapt, and grow.

Is there a trick to shifting our perspective on failure? Not really.

It comes down to vision.

From my experience, elite athletes, leaders, and the most successful people in the world fail forward because they stay focused on their vision with laser-tight precision, remaining relentless when working toward their possibilities.

Chapter 16

PATH TO SUCCESS

When 2014 flipped into 2015, I lived in Edmonton, AB. In addition to working toward my athletic goals, I contracted to help a startup company called SafeStart Education. Our goal was to educate all tenth-grade students stepping into the labor force with a safety curriculum helping to prevent human error. It was a noble effort to keep young people safe as they enter the workplace.

There were a few reasons for moving to Edmonton—it was an excellent opportunity to work in schools with young people, sharing my story, inspiring them to change their behavior with a proven safety-training process. It was also as far away from mountains as I needed to be at the time. While I wanted to be in the mountains more than anything,

I wasn't ready to be back. The mental and emotional toll of being near mountains—unable to use them the way I used to—was hard to bear.

My body, still in a state of disarray a year from my accident, had very little skin sensation below my waist. My balance and coordination—my athletic abilities—were severely diminished due to not feeling my legs or feet. My body continuously aching, my hand dexterity and strength weren't where I wanted them to be. I was walking, but I still needed a cane to let people know I was uneasy on my feet, as well as to assist my balance. I still had bowel, bladder, and sexual function deficiencies, and my physical strength was a fraction of what it used to be. I didn't even have the confidence to go to a regular gym because I could only lift the lightest dumbbells on the rack.

That said, I was motivated and working my butt off to get stronger. While I lacked the physical strength to work like I used to, the job with SafeStart stimulated me mentally unlike any other previous position. Working in high schools, teaching in classrooms and auditoriums was a humbling experience, and I was literally on the firing line with live rounds at the front of the classroom. I gained a new perspective and respect for schoolteachers—high school students aren't easy!

In my role with the company, I was a director of the athletics division. Tasked with delivering an industrial safety training program, I also tailored the teachings to prevent human error and enhance performance in student athletes. I was helping make decisions for the direction of the business under the leadership of the company's owners, as well as the executive director. However, my day-to-day duties mostly involved content creation, hiring and training staff, writing policies, and delivering the program.

It was awesome.

Working with a small, tightly-knit team, we were passionate about creating a program to support students across Alberta and beyond. If we succeeded in delivering the program to those who needed it, the business would thrive.

You may have heard this before—the path to success is never a straight line, but full of twists, turns, steps forward and steps backward. Great athletes, like great leaders, pick themselves up, failing forward time and time again by staying true to their vision. They stay fixated on their goals with laser focus—the end of the arrowhead.

Our goal with SafeStart Education was to shift behavior of the youth population entering the workforce to reduce the number of injuries for new and young workers—the highest risk group for injuries on any job site.

The mission was to help prevent accidents from happening to young people, and our vision was to spread the program across school systems so every young person could achieve his or her potential by accessing our life-saving technology. But, it wasn't that easy . . .

Roadblocks.

Operating in a public marketplace was, unfortunately, characterized with budget constraints and ever-changing government policy. Yes, our message and efforts were well received, but, in most schools, capacity to introduce new curriculum was constricted by limited teacher training opportunities, busy classroom schedules, and tightened spending. Logistically, it was a major challenge—we had plenty of interest, demand, funding, and support from school leaders and administrators, but the program only worked in a few schools.

Our company was propped up on speculative interest from the marketplace, but lack of ability for our customers to actually make the purchase and implement the program caused everything to come crashing down. We overestimated the market potential, overspent, and exhausted our resources. After two years of continuous effort, we closed the doors on the company, but not entirely.

All but one investor pulled out.

Our visionary, Larry Wilson, who created the SafeStart training process, remained true to our vision and, with the help of a smaller skeleton team, we set up a distribution company, separate from the mother company. We agreed to pay a royalty to keep using their intellectual property and, with that, we were off to the races.

Adjusting our strategy, we solved logistics problems, shortened teacher training, and reduced classroom time. Decreasing the price also helped, ramping up our selling efforts. We also looked at opportunities within the prison system in Alberta, and we pushed hard to get the program established as a widely accepted safety curriculum at a post-secondary, trade-school level. We were also expanding the offering for athletes, recognizing growth within the athletic injury prevention market.

After a year of operation under the new distribution company, we flatlined in the education market, unable to surpass strict policy regulations for curriculum and school budgets that were shrinking year after year. We saw some growth in sports, but the business was still suffering.

After one more year, we decided it was time to put SafeStart Education to bed.

We failed—again.

Why? The same problems we identified in the first two years. It didn't matter how much we improved the training, logistics, or our price—we couldn't break through policy. However, when things looked bleakest, it became apparent the way to succeed was to overcome a select few obstacles.

Toward the end of 2017, the idea for HeadStartPro Performance and Injury Prevention training was born. After addressing problems in front of us and knowing those obstacles were the way forward, our team went to work building a new program. Over the next twelve months, we redesigned our training to be performance focused. After all, we were in the business of preventing human error and injuries—if we could help people prevent making mistakes, they'd perform better and sooner at whatever they do.

Who could use improved performance? Who's driven by performance?

Athletes.

HeadStartPro now provides performance and injury prevention training to coaches and athletes across North America. It has become widely successful in achieving injury prevention results with teams recording between a 30-86% reduction in injuries, and they were winning more medals.

In retrospect, success with the company has been full of twists and turns, steps forward, and backward. We failed a few times and that, in the end, is why we succeeded. The lessons learned through failure along the way are the reasons we got it right.

How did we do it?

We kept coming back to these words . . .

Remember why you started.

We kept our vision to help young people achieve their potential with our life-saving technology on our radar. While the approach changed, the vision stayed the same—all we needed to do was change our strategy. The program is now available online at a price practically everyone can afford. We made the training accessible, affordable, and effective using an online platform.

We were also effective in influencing a behavioral change in young people by appealing to performance for motivation. No one really likes safety, but performance is something grabbing everyone's attention, especially athletes. By giving coaches and young athletes the tools to improve their game—which is what they really want—we sell them what they need—injury prevention. At the organizational level, athlete health, longevity, and safety are imperative, so injury reduction is a necessity.

The path to success is riddled with side steps and roadblocks. However, each of us must realize a step backward is still a step forward if you never stop working toward your goals. It's just the next step you need to take!

It's your opportunity to learn, adapt, and grow.

Setbacks help you identify skill gaps, highlighting where you can improve and achieve progress.

Remember, the reason why great athletes, leaders, and achievers of our time don't lose heart and persevere through the doldrums is because they stay gripped by their goals. They maintain laser-like focus on their vision to keep moving ahead.

Goal setting is critical for us as it is for athletes, and there's data to back it up. According to the Harvard Business Review, there's a strong correlation between setting goals and achieving success.

In 1979, interviewers asked new graduates from Harvard's MBA Program, "Have you set clear, written goals for your future and made plans to accomplish them?"

The results?

- 84% had no specific goals, at all.

- 13% had goals, but weren't committed to paper.

- 3% had clear, written goals as well as plans to accomplish them.

In 1989, interviewers again interviewed graduates of that class. You can guess the results . . .

- The 13% of the class who had goals were earning, on average, twice as much as the 84% who had no goals, at all.

- Even more staggering—the 3% who had clear, written goals were earning, on average, ten times as much as the other 97% *combined*.

Pretty alarming!

Currently, the study is under a bit of scrutiny because people question its validity since there was a study from Yale with almost identical findings in 1953.

Whether the study is entirely accurate or not, the numbers are staggering in favor of writing down goals, and having a plan in place to achieve them. If you've never set goals or written down your goals, I encourage you to spend time to reflect and plan with them in mind—make sure goals you set are specific, measurable, attainable, realistic, and timely (SMART goals).

For most of us, our goals over the next couple of years are pretty easy to consider—but, what about five-year goals?

The vision starts getting a bit foggier, doesn't it? That's why it's better to start with big-picture ideas and long-term goals for ten years, and beyond.

Starting with long-term goals makes your short-term goals clearer in the goal-setting process. For instance, once you set your ten-year goals with as much specificity as possible, when it comes to setting one, two, or five-year goals, you have to ask, "Is this getting me closer to my long-term vision?" If the answer is no, you know you need to take that goal out of the rotation—if yes, keep working hard toward it.

Chances are if you're reading this, you know things don't always go according to what we have in mind and, sometimes, things happen that are never part of the plan— like a broken neck. But, by establishing and focusing on our goals, we know where we're going, and we can get back on track. Of course, sometimes goals change, but never give up on a goal because of the time it's going to take—time is going to pass, anyway. So, you might as well be working toward something that truly lights the fire within, and is enough reason jump out of bed in the morning.

My goal of going to the Olympics changed dramatically from the time I was very young—from Olympian skier to coaching and, currently, when I might judge the freestyle ski events at the Olympic Games one day, representing Canada. The way I engage with the sport of freestyle skiing is very different now, but I'm still working my way up the ranks as a freeski judge. As long as I can, I'll keep judging, supporting the sport I love and, if I get to the Olympics, it'll be a dream come true.

But, you know—now that I think about it, it's not my top priority, anymore. I'm not sure because I know I have other possibilities. Let's face it—things change. Goals change. When they do?

Accept it, and move forward.

All we can do is remain focused on our long-term vision—the bigger the idea, the better. High-reaching goals, whether or not you're on target, produce similar results. When setting goals, aim high, and keep looking toward what is possible for you. Then, take action. Momentum becomes your ally as you make progress toward each, individual success.

It's all about possibilities . . .

Chapter 17

MINDSET

—Growth versus Fixed—

Remember my surgeon's words . . . "Mike, you should prepare yourself, you're probably never going to walk again . . ."

My world completely imploded in that moment, and I couldn't believe what I just heard—mostly because I didn't want to believe it. How could someone I just met tell me what the rest of my life was going to look like with such certainty?

How can anyone know what you're capable of except you?

They can't.

I mentored people who experienced spinal cord injuries, a few telling me they just knew walking was not something they would do again. Some give it a try and, sometimes, invest a ton of time and resources into learning to walk—in their hearts, however, they know it's something that might be unattainable. Often, they choose to set their sights on new possibilities, their focus becoming more about what they can do with their abilities rather than what they can't.

In my case, I had a feeling in the very core of my being the doctors were wrong. I still can't explain it to you to this day, but I just knew. There was certainly an element of stubbornness that helped—even so, I didn't want to believe the words. Something, though, was telling me they were wrong.

Imagine for a second . . . if I allowed the spinal specialist to tell me what my possibilities would be—or, rather, my impossibilities. Imagine I agreed with the doctors. Imagine I gave up on ever walking again in that instant. If I did those things?

I let them define my impossibility.

I can't say I would never have walked again for sure. But, I know damned right if I hadn't set my vision as well as setting massive milestone-like goals along the way and striving continuously toward my possibilities, I might not be upright today. I don't know for sure if I would have the abilities I do if I decided I wasn't supposed to have them.

Only you know your capabilities.

In 2018, I was looking for a new challenge. I felt like I plateaued in therapy, and I wasn't making physical gains—and, my quality of life suffered because of it. I actually noticed a regression in my strength and capacity, and I was starting to feel more pain on a more frequent basis. Life was becoming more of a challenge, so I knew I needed a new objective to conquer.

I discovered a race called the Red Bull 400, aptly named for its 400-meter course—or, about 437 yards—just over the length of four football fields. But, here's the catch—it's the steepest race in the world, the race is actually up an Olympic ski jump! The race really caught on since its inception in Austria in 2011, and now there are twenty events spanning three continents taking place at Olympic ski jumping sites.

To take on the Red Bull 400 race, I would run 400 meters on a thirty-seven degree incline from the bottom of a ski jump, straight to the top. Participants end up running up the equivalent of a forty-story building in a matter of minutes. It is a cardiovascular, leg burning, lung exploding, workout from the moment you start ascending the steep slope.

From what I learned, there are three types of participants in the Red Bull 400 events . . .

—Approximately 10-20% of people are there to compete. They're elite triathletes and marathoners of the world looking for the ultimate cross-training experience.

—Around 60-80% of the competition field are there for a challenge. They're the weekend warriors of the world, amateur athletes who train harder than most, seeking tremendous challenges such as the steepest running race on the planet.

—The other 10-20% see it as more of a gimmick. It tests them, pushing the limits of what might be physically possible. Some people in that category might come into the race not knowing what they're getting themselves into—their goal isn't a personal best, but simply to finish the race.

At the top of the ski ramp, participants often collapse, diving into the finish area, a small padded landing space. Some athletes walk it off, but some aren't so lucky. Much of the competitive population can't keep their breakfast down, vomiting from sheer exhaustion. In some cases, paramedics might need to give support as well as much needed hydration.

Either way, everyone's lungs were burning.

It sounded like a great challenge for an incomplete quadriplegic to me—so, the race became my possibility, keeping me motivated in training for months in advance of race day.

I drove out to Whistler, BC, to the beautiful Callaghan Valley—site of the Vancouver 2010 Winter Olympic Games ski jumping. It was August, and mountain meadows were in bloom, black bears speckling the hillsides as they grazed on berries and fresh green foliage. Interestingly, ski resorts are an ideal habitat for bears because of the wide-open ski runs where berries flourish.

As I approached the event venue, I began to feel nervous energy, knowing the race would test my abilities beyond any physical challenge I set for myself. The event was short, but I didn't know if my legs had it in them to climb all the way to the top.

Finally, when the venue first came into view, the butterflies in my stomach intensified. *What did I do!? Why did I decide to tackle this beast?*

In person, the hill was more daunting than I could have imagined. What if I fell? I wouldn't likely stop tumbling until I hit the bottom.

My race bib number placed in the first heat, so I wouldn't get a chance to see anyone run the slope before I was alongside my fellow competitors.

We lined up on the start line and, with the gun's resounding crack, we were off! I could hear the announcers voices above the chaos cheering us on.

The first 100 yards of the course was flat as I ran across what would be the ski jump finish area. As soon as I got beyond the flats, it steepened quickly, and I remember saying to myself, "Slow. Steady. One foot in front of the other . . ."

I had music playing in my headphones, angry hip-hop, keeping me in a steady rhythm, and I kept my head down. *Left foot. Right foot. Left foot, right foot* . . . I took a moment to look down from where I just departed, almost losing my balance, and the momentary lapse of focus nearly caused me to lose my footing, and teeter backward!

I threw myself onto the hill, grabbing the tall grass with both hands. I'm not sure what was worse—looking down and feeling a sense of vertigo, or looking up at how much of the formidable hill I still needed to climb. But, I kept going on my hands and knees.

I couldn't risk falling again.

At approximately two-thirds of the way into the race, the slope started to lessen as I crested the top of the ski jump's landing hill. The moment of reprieve, however, was short-lived because once I walked across the short, flat section at the top of the landing, I stepped onto the plywood surface of the ski jump. At one-to-two foot intervals, there were boards screwed into the plywood, resembling a ladder—or, rather, a stair climber from hell.

I continued telling myself to keep my mind off the slope, pushing my body to keep going. Back on my hands and knees as I made my way higher up the ramp, I knew I was almost there. *I can't fall now!*

Pausing just shy of the summit, my body screamed at me to stop—it was giving up, but my mind wasn't. I pushed the last few yards, stepping over the finish line, avoiding the pile up of bodies on the crash mats.

My lungs were on fire, my legs were shaking, but I made it!

My time?

Just under nine minutes—approximately six minutes behind the winners. I wasn't first, but I wasn't last! I landed somewhere in the middle of the pack and, to me, it was more than a victory. Just getting to the top made my heart explode with gratitude, adrenaline coursing through my veins. I was told I'd never walk again, and there I was—standing triumphant at the top of the steepest running race in the world!

It's worth mentioning again, exceptional athletes—like great leaders and high achievers—have an uncanny ability to lean consistently into and toward their possibilities versus impossibilities. They lean that way because they're exceptional at keeping their vision in mind.

We now know goal setting and vision are tokens of great leadership—but, an important addition to the leadership mix is belief. It's the foundation of all great leaders' mindsets because our beliefs influence our emotional states—and, as you know, emotions influence thoughts, and those thoughts influence behavior.

For instance, limiting beliefs can affect our behavior because they might hold us back from taking actions we would otherwise take if the belief weren't present. If I believed the doctors when they told me I'd never walk again? It wouldn't have served me. That kind of belief would have made my standing upright a less likely outcome. It would have held me back—especially when it came to challenges such as climbing the Red Bull 400 course.

I'm glad I didn't let doctors influence my mindset, or beliefs that day. I listened, but I wasn't going to jump to any conclusions, allowing them to dictate my possibilities—or, my impossibilities. The only person who knows what you're capable of is you—something to remember.

Choosing to believe our limitless possibilities are attainable is a mindset needing to be developed and nurtured. When we look at possibilities versus impossibilities on a spectrum, the polarity is evident—one end of the spectrum is positive, the other negative.

Everyone is born with the voice of positive self-talk. It's inside our heads telling us we're worthy, we have what it takes, we're enough, and we can believe in ourselves. But, we also have the voice of negative self-talk, self-doubt, self-loathing, self-pity, and scarcity. As a result, over time, our mindset changes, and we become more self-critical. In fact, we become so hard on ourselves, when we look in the mirror, if anyone ever talked to us the way we talk to ourselves, we'd never be friends with that person!

No way.

When we talk about possibilities versus impossibilities, we're essentially talking about having a growth versus a fixed mindset. According to world-renowned Stanford University Psychologist, Carol Dweck, author of the famous book, *Mindset, the new psychology of success,* with a growth mindset, people believe their most basic abilities can be developed through dedication and hard work—brains and talent are just the starting point. Such a view creates a love of learning, and essential resilience for great accomplishment.

A growth mindset leads to a desire to learn and, therefore, a tendency to:

- Embrace challenges

- Persist in the face of setbacks

- See effort as the path to mastery

- Learn from criticism

- Find lessons and inspiration from success of others

- Reach higher levels of achievement as a result.

Dweck also notes in a fixed mindset people believe their basic abilities, intelligence, and talents are merely fixed traits. They have a certain amount, and that's that—then, their goal becomes to look intelligent all the time, never the opposite. Why?

It makes them believe they're stupid, and that becomes fixed—and, no amount of effort will change it.

Interesting, isn't it?

A fixed mindset leads to a desire to look smart and therefore a tendency to:

- Avoid challenges

- Give up easily

- See effort as fruitless, or worse

- Ignore useful negative feedback

- Feel threatened by the success of others

- Plateau early, and achieve less than their full potential

If I were to ask you which mindset you have, what would you say?

I can hear you now . . . "Well, it depends—it depends on the activity, day and, sometimes, it depends on the hour. Even the minute!"

Know what I'd say? "You're absolutely right!"

We're not one or the other one hundred percent of the time, but we do tend to lean one way or the other—and, unfortunately, as we age, the voice of negative self-talk can become louder.

But, does it have to? Do we have to lean toward our impossibilities as we age?

I hope you agree with me when I say it does not.

We don't grow up a young dreamer saying, "One day, I'm going to grow up to be a failure!" And, we certainly don't say, "One day, I'm going to grow up to be in a wheelchair!"

When we're young, we have nothing but a growth mindset. The good news is if it changes at all, we can put in effort to develop it, thereby changing our mindset to be more growth oriented. It is possible. The best athletes and leaders do it, and some of the biggest companies in the world align themselves with athletes who have a growth mindset.

When I was in the hospital after breaking my neck, I was faced with numerous challenges. In physiotherapy, I had to relearn how to use my body, and I was starting from scratch.

Well, one day in physio, I was given simple instructions to roll over from my back to my front, then work my way up onto my hands and knees. It was a pivotal step in learning to walk because, if I were successful, I could isolate my hip joints—with the help of my physiotherapist—then, work on balancing from a kneeling position.

Rolling over was easy enough, but getting up to my hands and knees proved to be much more difficult. I tried repeatedly, failing over and over, and over again. I didn't have the strength in my arms to lift my torso off the mat.

As we neared the end of my one-and-a-half-hour physio session, I vividly remember my physiotherapist, Peter, saying to me, "It's okay if you can't right now—you're doing so well."

So . . . what was the only word you think I heard in that sentence?

That's right—can't.

I decided in that moment I could do it! I tried one last time, giving it everything I had. And . . .

I did it!

I pushed into the mat with all of my might, lifting myself up onto my hands and knees in a tabletop position! It was for only a moment before I collapsed, and Peter caught me before I went headfirst into the mat—but, I did it!

Hence—an epiphany.

I lay on the mat catching my breath. *If I can get through this, I can do anything!*

I'm not unique. We've all had 'ah-ha' moments. We've all had times in our lives when we're faced with a challenge for which we didn't possess the skills or qualities needed to overcome it. Even with such thoughts, it's good to remember times when you overcame a significant challenge when, at the time, you thought you didn't have what it took to succeed. Somehow, however, you're here. So, knowing that, think about . . .

—What did it take to move beyond the challenge?

—What did it take to succeed?

—Did you activate your growth mindset?

The truth is we're a balance of growth and fixed mindsets—and, as I mentioned, we tend to lean one way or the other. Your fixed mindset might be louder than your growth, and that's okay because we know now it's not fixed. With a bit of work and effort, you can shift from your fixed tendencies to a growth mindset.

Try to keep those 'ah-ha' moments in mind—the times you overcame significant obstacles requiring a growth mindset. You can find strength and self-confidence knowing you have what it takes to solve the next problem in your way. And, if there's a skill gap right now, it simply means you'll have to put in effort to learn new skills.

Usually, whether or not you achieve your possibilities doesn't come down to if it's physically possible, or if you possess the skill right now—it's the mindset you choose for your approach.

In 2019, I returned to the Red Bull 400 race in Whistler, and I ran it 1.5 minutes faster!

What's your next goal?

Chapter 18

IDENTITY

There I was, standing in front of a small classroom on Vancouver Island in the fall of 2017, and I was there to talk to a middle school class.

"Everyone," the teacher announced, looking expectantly at her students, "this is Mr. Shaw. We're lucky to have him in our class today! We're going to watch a documentary film featuring him called, *The Healing Agent*—and, he's going to talk with us about identity."

Ms. Burton and I talked briefly about what the message of my presentation should be, and we agreed identity would be a good topic. She was already talking about personal identity and self-confidence for much of the semester, and it seemed the perfect fit.

"Mr. Shaw's story is inspiring," she continued. "He had a difficult journey bringing him to us today." Again, she looked at her students, then began clapping. "Welcome, Mr. Shaw!"

I nodded, smiling. "Thank you, Ms. Burton. Speaking of identity, please call me Mike! And, thank you for the kind words—I hope I can deliver. After we watch the film, we'll get right into it . . ."

I hadn't planned much for the session with Ms. Burton's students. I was relatively new to the motivational speaking game, so I was volunteering my time. My thought was sometimes a free-flowing dialogue at the front of the room could take my audience to cool places in terms of motivation— especially with a group of middle schoolers!

I cued up my film entitled, *Mike Shaw, the Healing Agent.*

Chapters ago, I mentioned my two friends, Darren and Jan, who are filmmakers. During the two years following my accident, I worked tirelessly on a documentary film with them and, as the film came together and my recovery became more miraculous, Red Bull Media House picked it up, blowing away our wildest expectations! It's now on Red Bull TV, documenting my recovery from the time I was fully paralyzed. It features footage of my crash—that fateful moment changing my life forever. It's a powerful visual, especially for a group of preteens.

As the film came to an end, I was thinking about ways to capture the message of identity in my talk, and it occurred to me I'd been given that title—The Healing Agent, and it wasn't something I chose. It just sort of happened . . .

When we were pitching the documentary idea it was proposed as *Flipside, the Mike Shaw Story*, but it never flew, and Red Bull Media came back with *The Healing Agent*.

Cued by their teacher, the kids applauded when the film credits rolled. "Thank you, thank you! You guys are fantastic!" I made best use of a brief pause. "You know," I continued, "I never thought of it before, but, when it comes to identity, I didn't think of myself as The Healing Agent—but, it's not far off the mark. Since my accident, I chose to help all sorts of people, mentoring those who have spinal cord injuries so they can heal through their physical, mental, and emotional pain."

Well, that was quite the epiphany, but I didn't stay on the point for long. "What makes up your identity," I asked.

Surprisingly, the kids started shouting out words such as dancer! Soccer player! Gamer! Artist! Brother! Sister! Student! Immigrant! But, one student said something totally blowing me away. "I am kind . . ."

"Yes! You're all of those things, but you are also kind. And, you're a whole lot more than labels! Let's look at it like this—who was I, Mike Shaw, before and after the crash?" I wasn't sure where I was going, but I wrote my name on the chalkboard, right up at the top, center. Then, I wrote 'before' on the left and 'after 'on the right, separating them into two columns. "Who was Mike Shaw before the accident," I asked.

"Skier! Athlete! Coach! Adrenaline Junkie! Adventurer! Son! Brother!" Each answer was exactly correct, and the kids were onto something. There was a time in my life if someone asked, "Who is Mike Shaw," without fail, my name and 'skier' would be used in the same sentence. "Mike Shaw is a skier . . ." And, it would rarely go beyond two sentences. "Mike Shaw is from Vernon. He's a skier . . ."

But, once we got past the obvious labels, we needed to dig a little deeper. So, we added friend, responsible, kind, honest, loving, and trustworthy to the list.

"Okay—that ought to do it—so, who was I after the crash?"

That one stumped them a bit.

"How about this—we know I wasn't a skier anymore." So, I put a big 'X' through the word skier. "I wasn't an athlete anymore, or a coach—and, I definitely wasn't an adrenaline junkie like I used to be." I continued to cross off all those words. "I might have been adventurous, but I wasn't much of an adventurer, anymore . . . " That word also got the ax.

So, who was I?

"I'll tell you who I think I was after the crash." I started writing on the board, "I was injured. I was in a wheelchair. I was a quadriplegic. I was paralyzed. In the weeks following the accident in the hospital, I started inspiring others. I realized I was still compassionate, I still had my bad sense of humor, I was reliable and grateful, and I still had my integrity."

Then, I asked, "who am I now? I don't look injured, and I don't have a wheelchair. I might be an incomplete quadriplegic, but you'd never know it. I'm not completely paralyzed . . ."

I crossed off all of those words on the board, left with friend, responsible, kind, honest, loving, trustworthy, son, brother, compassionate, humor, reliable, grateful, and dependable.

I turned from the chalkboard to face them. "Guys and girls—we're so much more than our labels. If you do a bit of digging, you're so much more below the surface than the things you do, your hobbies, or your sports. You have an incredible foundation that makes you—well . . . you. Once you know that, you get to choose your labels, as well as things you want to do . . ."

Ms. Burton's students helped illuminate a struggle I was dealing with—moving beyond being stuck, hopelessly missing my old labels such as 'Mike Shaw, the Skier.'

The fact is those kids aren't any different than you or I—all of us are much more than our labels. We're more than our jobs, hobbies, or titles to which we attach value. Most of us haven't given much conscious thought to our own identities, and we inadvertently shift and shape our identity based on desires, experiences, beliefs, and labels we give ourselves. To some, identity is something we inherit, an innate quality we can't change—or, is difficult to change. Most of us unintentionally give our labels the permission to play the enormous role in our identities which can be terribly problematic, especially when facing transition or trauma.

When was the last time someone asked you what you do, leaving the question open ended? Chances are you answered with your job title, or what you do for a living. You might say a sport or a hobby if you spend most of your time doing it, but it's most likely your job. So, it's no surprise we prime ourselves to believe such labels make us who we are. I'm not saying they're meaningless labels—after all, we put a lot of time and effort into our careers and hobbies. They're important, but there's a lot more going on under the surface comprising our identity.

What I realized in the middle school classroom was our core values and characteristic traits are a more accurate definition of our identities. Following my accident, I struggled with the loss of my big picture titles, but I also knew I was so much more than just a skier. Deep down, I was sure about who I was, and I'd never been more confident. I realized, by grounding and getting in touch with the foundation of my identity, I could choose my new labels with certainty I would remain strong at my core. That's important because you never know if the label will be there forever.

Our labels or titles—whether we choose them or not—are the most malleable components of our identities. They're often transient and, when facing a transition of losing a label or enduring a trauma such as divorce, retirement, or disease, we must return to who we are at our core.

Loss of identity can leave us feeling stuck. It can be devastating to feel as if we lost our purpose, and it can affect anyone. Even a recovering addict will feel the void of losing his or her identity—in addition to withdrawal symptoms—because they lost a big part of who they perceive themselves to be. They sacrifice relationships because they often have to give up friends if they want to give up their addictive habits—a huge shift often riddled with grief. But, remember—if you're feeling stuck, know you're so much more than your labels, and you can choose new big picture ideas, new labels, and a new purpose to ignite your soul.

I took this concept and started working for a Post-Traumatic Stress Recovery Program, making the most of my opportunity to share my good fortune, as well as mentor ex-military, police officers, firefighters, and paramedics suffering from PTSD after leaving their careers. Not only that, most of them suffered from perceptually losing their identities. All they knew was a life of service, one weighted heavily by their careers, resulting in a huge hole in their identities. For many of those men and women, loss of identity spawned and exacerbated issues such as abandonment, abuse, and addiction.

It was in those stress-recovery sessions the identity audit was born . . .

It involves a deep dive into your core values, traits, and characteristics by taking an introspective look at your personality and what matters most to you in this world— in the process, you'll realize you're much more than you think. Try it! It doesn't matter if you experienced trauma, or are going through a major life transition such as divorce or retirement. By taking stock and auditing your core beliefs, it can build great confidence by giving you a foundation from which to grow. Getting in touch with your inner self is imperative to free your mind, letting go of labels that aren't serving you, or grief you might hold when losing someone important.

Here are some core values I identified with others:

—Accountable, Authentic, Adventurous

—Caring, Committed, Compassionate, Courageous

—Dependable, Diverse

—Empathetic

—Gracious, Generous

—Honest, Humble, Humorous

—Possessing Integrity

—Kind

—Loving

—Loyal

—Motivated

—Open-minded, Optimistic

—Positive

—Passionate

—Reliable, Resilient, Respectful, Responsible

—Serving, Strong, Sympathetic

—Trustworthy

Some of those values, traits, and characteristics might stand out to you. Though the list isn't exhaustive, it gives you a glimpse into your own identity, and who you are at your core.

A recurring value kept surfacing repeatedly for men and women in the PTSD clinics. Each who looked inward and asked tough questions, assessing their core values, unanimously decided service made up a major part of their identities. They valued service, dedicating their careers and lives to helping others. It may have been service to their country or community, but it always came back to service above self.

We opened the door so those men and women could keep fulfilling their purpose—and, *purpose* is an important part of who we are. We're longing for belonging and influence in life—we long to have and connect with our purpose. For those trauma survivors with PTSD, their purpose was always to serve others.

Much like misconstruing labels as our identities, there's a misconception your purpose needs to be in line with your job.

Nope.

You could make money creating and selling widgets, then use your financial resources to create a better life for your family, do the things you love to do, or donate to charity—or, to do something like support your church. You get the idea. If purpose and career align, great—but, if not, no problem. We can still live out our lives with our truest identity in line with our purpose.

In the PTSD clinics, we discovered the participants' desires to serve others was something they could still undertake. They could carry on fulfilling their identity, as well as their purpose, only in a slightly different way with a different label. They could direct their efforts toward their families—or, volunteer in their communities. They could become the best team players in their new jobs, supporting wider initiatives of companies for which they work. By connecting with their truest selves, they realized their identities weren't only intact, they were stronger. They could confidently take on life, staying true to themselves, finding happiness in the days ahead.

In some cases, the identity was a negative. The flip side of losing something you were proud of is losing something you loathe. The question is how do you get rid of those negative titles? How do you get rid of labels we give ourselves such as too fat, too thin, too short, loser, failure, or unworthy? Well, the process stays the same—it just might take more of the introspective work for someone who's feeling fixed, listening to the devil rather than the angel. You might choose to go deeper by auditing your thoughts, feelings, and beliefs, paying close attention to your conscious mind to unlearn negative patterns. It takes effort, but it's an audit of your awareness.

On my last night in the hospital at G.F. Strong, I was slowly but surely packing things in my room—it was late, so visitors had long since gone home, and I was staying in the independent wing of the hospital ward for my final few days at GFS which was the quiet end of the hall.

Suddenly, I heard a voice call to me from outside my room. Surprised to hear anyone there that late, I went to see who it was.

"Mike! Mike! Are you awake?"

I poked my head into the hallway, "Steve! What's up? What are you doing up so late?"

Steve is an incomplete quadriplegic who has limited use of his arms or hands. He was approaching sixty years old, almost at retirement, injured mountain biking. He had no family support, no retirement savings, and no hope.

"Well, I'm having trouble sleeping—anyway, I know it's your last night, so I wanted to come by . . ."

"Man, thank you. It's slow, but I'm packing up my things. I have to stop every few minutes because of the pain, but I'm making progress." I was making small talk, but that wasn't why Steve came to chat.

"I just wanted to say . . . it's impressive. You know—what you're able to do. You've come so far—and, I just wanted to say congratulations." He paused trying to find his next words.

"Steve, you don't have to say that. I'm just lucky. Well, arguably the luckiest of the unlucky—no one is lucky to break their neck, but, nevertheless, lucky. Anyone in here would do the same thing given the chance."

That's when it got dark.

"I know. I know . . ." Steve's voice broke. "I would if I could, too. I just . . . I just can't take it. I hate this body. I hate being trapped, and I want out. I've been trying to stack my pain meds, so I can painlessly leave this world."

Whoa! I didn't know it at the time, but I was about to do my first identity audit.

Steve wasn't the most liked person in the hospital. He was loud and vocal about his distaste for his injury, as well as being confined to the hospital. It wasn't his life, and he let everyone know. One-night, I rolled by the nurses' station to let someone know his call light was on above his room, and I'll never forget seeing them in the break room—one pulled the short straw, and had to help Steve.

The problem was he didn't want to help himself, so no one wanted to help him. He treated nurses like shit, showing little or no gratitude. Whenever asked how his day was going, he'd say, "It's fucked. I'm completely fucked . . ."

That night in the hall outside my room, I got to know a bit more about him. "Man—that's heavy. There's got to be something to live for . . ."

It was then he spilled his guts. "There's not—I hate this body. It's not my body. I don't have a family, or anyone to help me. My kids haven't talked to me in years—I was never a good dad. I don't have a place to live. I don't have a job. I don't have any money." A pause. "I used to be physical—it's what I did. I used to work for a living. I used to be a fighter. Now, what am I? Nothing. What's the point?"

"Steve, you're a fighter—and, this is the biggest fight of your life. All of those things are difficult I know, but you're going to get through. If it's not working out right now, it just means it's not finished yet because things will always work out. You'll find somewhere to live. We can't stay locked up in here forever . . ."

It didn't stick on the first try. "But, the nurses are no help—my social worker is useless, and can't find any affordable or accessible housing. I'd take either one of those at this point . . ."

"Man, you have to start taking steps to make it work out. Getting down on the people who're trying to help you, won't do any good. Remember, you're a fighter! What kind?"

"I was a boxer . . ."

"There! There you have it! You're still a fighter, but it's just a different fight. You're going punch for punch with a spinal cord injury. Are you going to lose the fight?"

Then, I saw it. His expression changed as he shifted forward in his wheelchair. "No—I always hate losing a fight."

"This isn't something I'd wish on my worst enemy, but our only way out is if we fight. You haven't lost as much as you think. Your spirit is still the same . . ."

"I hope you're right . . ."

"Me, too. But, I'm gonna come back here and, when I do, I'm going to check on you. Deal?"

"Yeah, man—I'd like that. Anyway, I just wanted to say congrats. And, thank you—thank you for this conversation. You've always been so nice to me . . ."

"Anytime—have a good night, and keep fighting."

By the time we were done talking, I was spent. My neck was aching like crazy, and I collapsed onto the bed, drifting off to sleep, thankful for all I had—not what I lost.

I kept my promise, checking in on him a few weeks later. "How's it going, man? Still fighting?"

"Still fucked!" Then, he smiled, holding a small stack of papers on his lap.

"But you know what this is? It's my approval for affordable, accessible housing. I'm moving out of the hospital, man!"

I'll never forget him . . .

Since PTSD clinics, I've worked with individuals on a one-on-one basis with the identity audit, presenting my findings from 'Jane and John Doe's' identity work at the University of Manitoba Case Management Symposium in Winnipeg in 2018. As a result, I built the exercise into leadership and team-building workshops for corporate groups, and it's become a big part of what I do as well as who I am. Whenever I feel as if I'm lost or stuck, longing for my old body or old identity—Mike Shaw the Skier—I always come back to my foundation where I know I'm much more than any one of those labels. Skier, coach, adventurer, or speaker . . .

I enjoy being a professional speaker, reaching and connecting with international audiences. I like the label, and it sticks with me. I like that I'm working toward being an author as I write these words. I like that I was given the title, Mike Shaw the Healing Agent. I like those things, and I like choosing the weight they hold with my identity. I control my attachment to the titles—and, if gone tomorrow, it would be difficult. I might feel lost for a while, but I'm confident I'll always return to my core, knowing I can weather the storm.

I know I'm here to help others—ever since I started to coach skiing, I've been good at and passionate about helping. This book is simply an extension of that—the medium has changed, but driving values at my core stay the same.

We're so much more than our labels.

Chapter 19

TEAMWORK

Why do you think they call it teamwork, and not team-take-it-easy? There's only one reason—because it takes work to succeed at almost anything. As my grandma used to say, "If a job is worth doing, it's worth doing right." In order to do something right, you need to put in effort, and it helps if you choose to work hard. No matter how good you are, hard work always prevails in the face of challenge and adversity, especially when your team backs you and your vision.

I've been on teams my entire life. Freestyle skiing is an individual sport and, while it might seem counterintuitive, it's heavily team reliant. My freestyle ski team shared a vision—our unanimous goal was to become a professional skier, standing on the podium.

There were different skiing disciplines represented on
our team including big air, slope style, half-pipe, moguls, and
big mountain. It didn't matter who was in which stream—
all of us were working toward the same thing. Even in an
individual sport, we knew we would go further together than
trying it on our own. Here's the thing—if you want to go fast,
go alone.

If you want to go far, you need a team.

In G.F. Strong, while fighting in the trenches of my
recovery from SCI, I had a team of professionals supporting
me, backing my vision to walk out of the hospital. I was
very much the team captain in control of my own destiny,
as well as the person responsible for setting the team vision.
However, I worked with my therapists, taking their advice,
considering what they had to say before we collectively
agreed my vision of walking out of the hospital was realistic.

Once we shared that goal, progress started to ramp
up. I showed up every day, putting in my full effort—and,
I worked hard, the whole team reciprocating. Work ethic is
contagious, and I truly feel my therapists worked as hard
for me as I did for them. I thanked my team for every small
victory because, without them, I couldn't get where I wanted
to go. Even if I did, it wouldn't have happened as fast.

The people with whom you choose to surround yourself
become your team. The people you spend the most time
with and lean on in times of need should also be helping you
get to your next level. Josh Dueck was one of those people
for me.

When I moved home to Vernon, I tried to spend as much
time as I could with him, learning not only about his physical
triumphs—like winning the Paralympics and being the first
person to back flip a sit-ski—but, also to talk about the

mental and emotional growth he experienced after breaking his back. I chose to be around people whom I knew could elevate me to the level I envisioned myself, and beyond.

I also spent as much time as I could with my close friend, Calum Lloyd, because he was working on his MBA, striving for continuous improvement. When I ultimately moved to Edmonton, it was to work with Larry Wilson—an incredibly successful entrepreneur. Then, there was Doug Nelson—a wise man who holds a Ph.D. in Education Design—heading up a team of talented young people committed to growing a budding business.

I connect with people all over the world who share similar goals, and similar journeys as my own. The SCI club is reserved for the elite, but no one wants an invitation—and, thanks to my SCI, I had the good fortune to meet incredible people who also experienced paralyzing injuries.

You might remember I struggled at the Wings for Life World Run, but came out so far ahead of anything I thought possible. In 2016 and 2017, I fell short of my goals in the race, but, in 2018, I achieved my goal of running 7.5 miles—12.5 kilometers. In doing so, I raised money personally for the charity, raising awareness for spinal cord injury. However, if I wanted to make a bigger impact, I needed a bigger team.

Then, in 2017, I met someone from Halifax, Nova Scotia who would change my life in a very positive way, reshaping the entire Wings for Life World Run event across Canada— Jim Mullan. A quadriplegic, he broke his neck in a diving accident while on tour with Canadian hip-hop artist and icon, Classified—Jim played bass, and keyboard.

Talk about hard! Imagine not being able to use your arms or hands as a musician!

I connected with Jim on a deeper level, and with deeper understanding of the challenges we faced faster than I had with any other person dealing with a spinal cord injury. I never met anyone whose outcome from a cervical spinal cord injury was so similar, our neurological and neuropathic pictures uncannily alike. Our surgeries were the same, and our scars look like twins.

During a phone call in the summer of 2017, Jim and I were talking about the Wings for Life race taking place every May. "It's a totally cool event," I told him. "Maybe it's something you should do—for me, the race acts as a benchmark for physical progress. The run's a test of how my body's doing, and if I'm recovering. As time goes on farther from my injury date, physical progress is hard to see . . ."

"Love it! How do I get involved?"

"The race is also cool because you can do it anywhere— it's an App Run now!" That meant anyone can do the run using a Wings for Life App on a smart phone. "Just log in and register on the app. On race day, the phone starts tracking your progress using its GPS—it's weird because you'll hear the catcher car coming over your headphones as it gets closer and closer."

"That's so cool! I'm in! Imagine if we could get enough people together using the app to log enough kilometers to run across the country."

I was stunned. "What did you just say?"

"I said, imagine . . ."

"No! I heard you! It's brilliant!"

"You're damn right it is. You'll be team captain West, and I'll be team captain East."

The gears began to turn.

We discussed the idea at length, then got off the phone with brimming enthusiasm, but didn't do anything about it for months.

At the turn of the new year in 2018 and as the race approached, I reached out to the event organizers, pitching the idea of acquiring social media support to build the team. After all, if we wanted to hit our goal, we needed to get enough people together on the app to run over 3500 miles— or, 5500 kilometers—the distance from Vancouver, BC, to Halifax, NS.

It's a massive understatement to say convincing nearly 1000 people to run would be an arduous task—we didn't have that many friends! It would be next to impossible to accomplish by simply calling around—but, in my mind, we had to start somewhere, then it would grow.

So, I went online to set up a team page on the Wings for Life website, then called Jim. "I did it! I started the team! Let's do it, you and me—team captains. Are you on board?"

"Hell, yes!"

It was already late January when I started the team and, over the next four months, Jim and I started recruiting like crazy. We hit up everyone in our networks who would join, reaching out to everyone we knew who was affected by SCI. Jim leveraged his connections with Classified to get media appearances on CBC, and I hit up local newspapers and journalists. Our combined effort gathered just over 100 people on the virtual start line in 2018. Collectively we logged just over 400 miles—700 kilometers!

It was a start.

I can't say for sure, but I think it was the team behind me helping me in 2018. The collective consciousness and collective stoke of everyone on our team from coast to coast helped fuel my fire so I could crank out over 7.5 miles that day. I knew it before, but, I really knew it then—the power of a team is incredible.

If you want to go far, you need a team.

After the race in May of 2018, the amazing people at Wings For Life Canada took notice of Jim's and my efforts. Together, we identified a bunch of other bad-ass spinal cord injury survivors—warriors—setting out to grow the team. Our communication strategy was far better with the help of the pros—Christina Krcevinac at Red Bull helped promote the event by getting coverage on breakfast television shows, news broadcasts, print media, news articles, and all social media channels. Our team expanded to include every single runner in Canada who supported the charity event!

On May 8, 2019, we had over 700 people lined up on the virtual start line, logging miles, raising funds and much needed awareness for spinal cord injury research. Jim and I put forward great physical efforts running a respective 5 and almost 8 miles, but our 700+ teammates collectively ran just over 3000 miles. We almost reached our goal, but, more important, our team helped researchers around the world get one step closer to finding a cure, as well as better treatments for spinal cord injuries.

We need to find a cure.

I wouldn't wish spinal cord injury on my worst enemy—it's devastating, and not only for the person who has the injury, but for families and loved ones, too. It's a ripple effect—no one person gets affected by SCI. Your inner circle, outer circle, your community—everyone feels it.

'Traumatic' is an understatement.

In 2020, I'm confident we'll reach our goal and, if not, we'll keep working at it for years to come. We'll keep #teamcoast2coast going strong until we achieve the ultimate goal, finding a cure or treatment for SCI. This is one of the greatest teams I've ever been a part of, and I'm grateful for every person who joins, working toward our collective vision.

So . . . what should you look for in your team?

A team is a stable and bound group of individuals interdependent in achieving a shared goal. The best teams are those building relationships based on trust, and they practice together, win together, and fail together. The best teams know impressive teams are made up of impressive individuals. If you're impressive, you can be sure the person beside you, shoulder-to-shoulder, is also impressive. You hold each other to that standard.

Your team doesn't have to be traditional in the sense of the word. Your team doesn't need to wear the same colors, or work at the same job, or share the same hobbies. Sometimes, choosing your team simply means choosing your people. Who do you want around you? Do they support you? Do they share the same goals, drive, and work ethic? If not, maybe you need to make some subs—choosing people for your personal team should be done with great intention.

Sometimes, we don't get to choose our team. In some team environments, we're chosen to hold roles or support others whom we may not like. In such situations, whether it's at work, sport, or in life, how we handle ourselves matters, and finding common ground is key.

What are the values of your team, and how can you align yourselves with those in mind? People are different, but, if you find everyone values integrity, define the integrity of the team. Connect, build trust, and then set the vision. Determine your goals, objectives, and outcomes based on that shared vision.

Remember—it's called teamwork, not team take it easy. Challenge every team player to show up in your life. What will it take to get you where you want to go?

Work.

What is hard work?

It's your ability to put in a great deal of directed effort and endurance. Hard work requires discipline and determination. Consistency might waver slightly, but, if you have a good work ethic, you intrinsically connect work with rewards, and hold yourself to a standard not permitting laziness. The way forward is discipline, determination, and unrelenting consistent effort.

So, what does it *really* mean to work hard?

Well, it means showing up early and staying late. It means being present, putting in extra reps, and doing as much or more than your teammate next to you.

The late Kobe Bryant had one of the most remarkable work ethics in the entire NBA. His tenacity and drive were hard to emulate, and he intimidated other players on and off the court, living up to his name, Black Mamba.

Before games, as opposing players rolled into the Staples Center for pregame workouts, some noticed Kobe practicing game-time moves with full intensity on the court. Those same players, finishing their workouts over an hour later, walked out of the dressing rooms, hearing the echo of a basketball coming from the gym.

Kobe.

A few thought it foolish—certainly, he'd burn out, wouldn't he? Nope.

He ran over his opponents.

Kobe led the L.A. Lakers to five NBA championships with that intensity. He holds the Laker's franchise records in most-ever points, games played, and rebounds. He was a lethal weapon on the court and, while his ability to drain baskets baffled some of the best defenders in the game, he was also second in assists in franchise history. Kobe was a team player. He brought his team up. His work ethic and intensity fueled the fire of his entire team.

In January, 2020, basketball and the sports world lost a legend, but Kobe will live on in every athlete he ever inspired—even right here in the pages of this book.

It's called teamwork, not team take it easy, and your team will elevate you as much as you elevate them. If you have the luxury, choose your teammates wisely. If you don't, show them the way by doing the extra reps—like Kobe. Create trust by finding the values you share, creating the team vision together, and relying on each and every team member. Keep each other accountable, and remember . . .

Impressive teams are made up of impressive individuals.

Chapter 20

Gifts and Perspective—The Grief Journey

My TED Talk.

I never felt so sick to my stomach, and it was all I could do to keep from tossing my cookies. My girlfriend, Jocelyn, sat with me backstage in the green room, trying to calm me down, but I was too revved up—nothing but a bundle of nerves. I never felt such pressure, not in all of my time participating in skiing competitions.

I worked for over a year, and it came down to that moment. After applying, I put six months of work into the project before I was granted a spot on stage. I conducted interview after interview, putting countless hours into research. I wrote and rewrote my script, refining my message with every crumpled piece of paper in the trashcan. I performed at every rehearsal. I spent weeks memorizing what I was going to say, and I only had one shot.

I had to get it right.

I compare doing a TED talk to writing a thesis paper— I poured my lifeblood into the project, but, rather than handing in a paper at the end of the project term, I had to stand on stage, performing my talk to the world. No rewrites. No do-overs.

I had one chance.

Not only was there a lot of pressure to perform, my talk needed to provide a solution to one of the world's tough, tangible, specific, and universal problems. In other words, it needed to help humanity by providing an unmistakable remedy to a challenge all of us face. It needed to push the needle toward a better world.

The Queen Elizabeth Theatre in Vancouver, BC, holds slightly over 2700 seats—granted, a few were empty, but that didn't help calm my nerves. I was preparing to go on stage at the TEDx Stanley Park conference—an event among the top ten largest TEDx events held worldwide. A one-day event, the audience doubles the size of the TED week-long conferences.

To me, it was like the Olympics of public speaking. I was about to do my final run in the biggest event of my life.

No wonder I was nervous!

Instinctively, I fell back on my training as a freestyle skier. "Just stay here with me and listen," I commented to Jocelyn.

"Okay—but, don't worry. You know this! You've been through it a thousand times, and it's like muscle memory at this point . . ."

And, that's what I needed—that little bit of confidence.

I proceeded to close my eyes, visualizing 'my run,' Jocelyn patiently listening like she'd done countless times before.

As I spoke, I went through the motions in my mind, what it would be like to walk out on stage, every step I would take while standing on the red carpet—the red circle, symbolic of ideas worth sharing. I visualized every motion, every word start to finish, and I even visualized a standing ovation. You know—what it would feel like to share my story with thousands of people. Bow. Exit, stage left.

"When you walk out, walk with power," my speaking coach, Lucas, told me. "Walk with purpose. With every step, you'll feel your nervous energy and intensity shooting out of your feet like lightning bolts into the floor. Shrug the nerves off with every arm swing, getting more powerful with every stride . . ."

Boy, did that help! I never felt more ready, and more powerful. I felt as if I were an athlete in the starting gate again, going through the final few words of advice with my coach.

Then, I heard the conference producer, Roger, call my name. "Mike Shaw with his talk, Grief Happens . . ."

It was time.

I walked on stage, sending the nervous energy into the floor like Lucas instructed. I looked out at the crowd beyond the glare of the spotlights on me, and I could see my people in the audience. I was about to deliver the most difficult and most influential presentation of my entire life . . .

My TED talk.

"When you lose someone or something that matters," I began, "grief happens—it hurts. It's easy to feel lost, to lose motivation, and to feel angry. But, if you spend too much time in the darkness of grief, depression can set in—and, it's easy to get stuck. To lose your spark. Your passion for life.

When you experience grief, will you get *stuck*, or will you take back *your* life? Grief hit me so hard—yet, I'm here to share what I learned hoping you, too, can overcome grief like I did . . ."

In front of over 2500 people, I continued, vividly describing the catastrophic accident that changed my life, ripped away my independence, my career, my love for skiing, and almost everything I knew. "Have you ever felt like you hit rock bottom? Deep hopelessness? Despair," I asked the crowd. "With time, I realized the human emotion of grief is something we share. *Grief happens* . . .

My feelings weren't so different from someone sad for reasons like the end of a dream, financial ruin, disease, or divorce. It isn't always sudden, like the microsecond my neck broke—but, it can be, such as the unexpected loss of a loved one.

There's a ripple effect, too. I'll never forget my mom's tears, or my dad's brave face—my loss was their loss.

Grief happens. The causes vary, but the feelings are universal . . ."

In the process of conceptualizing, researching, and writing my talk, I had deep discussions with numerous people, asking all sorts of questions. I talked to people who were grieving from divorce or broken hearts—losing the lives they were supposed to have. People who were feeling lost in retirement, longed for a purpose. I talked to people who were battling disease—some were winning, some weren't.

Countless paraplegics and quadriplegics were grieving the loss of their physical bodies—something I knew well. I talked to people who lost loved ones in ways I could only imagine in my worst nightmares. In fact, I met people so deeply entrenched in their grief journey, I had a hard time finding words to help them heal.

One of my close friends recounted her dad and brother burning to death in a fiery crash as she watched from a bluff overlooking the runway, the plane engulfed in flames. Her brother, closer to the blaze, crouched in the gravel beside the plane after repeatedly reaching into the cockpit to try to pull his brother from the fire. His arms were badly burned by the time he realized it was futile—his brother and dad were already gone. Their lives, as well as the lives of their family members would never be the same.

As though it were placed there for him, where the brother crouched, he found a pen in the sand—it was his dad's, most likely jettisoned from his shirt pocket. He picked it up and, at twenty-six years old, he knew he had to fill the shoes of his lost family members, running the family business.

One mother grieved the loss of her son's suicide in their home. She and her husband got the call one morning after they went to work. In that conversation, I had a hard time finding the words—but, when I did, they seemed to help. Even a mother, completely tormented with grief, could find some peace in the love and gratitude for her son.

My words resonating, most made it into the talk. Her son was a big part of the final presentation reaching over 40,000 people in the grips of grief. Now, she's an advocate for youth mental health and suicide prevention, her son's legacy living on.

With every conversation, I got one step closer to the TEDxSP stage to share my ideas with the world—and, I knew the ideas were unique.

I struggled with grief and despair following my accident. I lost so much, and it felt as if my world were ripped away from me. However, where others' losses were permanent, mine was different—I lost things I'd never get back, such as freestyle skiing, the love of my life. It hurt, but I was also given a gift—hope. My body was getting better. I had no idea when—or, if—my healing journey would end and, with every bit of recovery I experienced, I felt an overwhelming sense of gratitude. And, it was gratitude fueling my fire for progress and healing.

More important, gratitude helped me change my perspective. Perception is how we understand things that happen to us, and we decide what those events mean to us physically, mentally, and emotionally.

There were times I felt angry because I broke my neck, but, objectively speaking, breaking my neck was out of my control. It happened, and I couldn't do anything to change it after the fact—but, my anger was by choice.

When you ask yourself how you can view adversity in a positive way—or, what you can be thankful for, perspective automatically shifts. For me, I chose to seek gifts. I chose to seek things for which I could be most grateful, and doing so helped me let go of my anger and sadness.

On stage, my words flowed with heartfelt emotion . . .

"When I thought about perspective, I thought about skiing. Standing atop high mountain peaks, feeling weightless in free-fall, or soaring twenty or thirty feet high off an eight-foot jump—they're the most amazing feelings! Hard feelings to lose . . . and, the thought I might not ski again was devastating.

But, I decided to change my perspective.

It occurred to me my emotional pain was directly proportionate to the joy and love I felt, and I couldn't feel so low without once feeling so high.

My loss really mattered.

Then, grief revealed a gift. Experiencing those highs was a gift—and, the lows gave me greater emotional capacity to appreciate the highs. Grief was validation. I had something in my life that mattered so much it hurt to lose. Now, I'm forever grateful to have had skiing in my life.

It's tough to talk about, but I knew I could turn the tables on grief and, with effort, I could choose gratitude. I'm not talking about blind, gushy optimism—I'm talking about putting in effort to cope with my grief, and move forward. Choosing gifts and perspective.

Gratitude.

I chose to be grateful I had skiing in my life, rather than fixating on all I lost. To this day, I'm forever grateful for skiing because it gave me more in life than it ever took away in trauma.

When you feel grief, you, too, can turn the tables by trying a different perspective. You can activate gratitude to help you heal. I'm not saying it's easy—especially when you're in a dark place, facing an uncertain new reality. Remember the gratitude triggers? Try them, or another way to feel thankful.

Today, I'm grateful every day because when I experience setbacks, which we all do, I'm often reminded about my losses—my ability to get unstuck falls back on gratitude.

For me, gratitude provides perspective, helping me to heal mentally and emotionally so I can focus on doing the work to heal physically."

I paused, focusing on the audience. "You *can* take back your life," I told them. "But, it won't be easy. Things won't suddenly be sunshine and rainbows—grief won't go away overnight, and there will be setbacks. Heck, I'm not convinced grief ever fully goes away when the loss is significant. When you feel pain, try a different perspective—you had someone or something in your life that mattered so much, it hurts to lose. But, remember—treasured memories are gifts—you *can* be forever grateful.

What if we look at it like this—our lows, the pain or hopelessness, give us greater emotional capacity to appreciate *new* highs. Trust you will heal, and you can live a full life after grief."

I felt the audience listening to every word, hoping they'd be willing to give gratitude a try. "Finally," I continued, "make a commitment to yourself that you'll *activate gratitude* to help *you* heal. Practice feeling grateful everyday, and BOOM! Gratitude triggered!

Whether grief tests you or not, your life will be better for it. If it does, remember grief happens, and don't get stuck. Find gratitude in the darkness, and take back your life!

If I can, so can you . . ."

What a powerful moment! When I walked off stage at TEDx Stanley Park, I was filled with gratitude, grateful for every step I took to be on that stage, literally and figuratively.

I know I'm lucky—yes, I lost a lot, but I'm lucky because, in the end, I had an extraordinary recovery from my injury. I'll never have the coordination to ski like I used to, but I'm very fortunate. I am in the spinal cord injury club and, as a result, I've seen a spectrum of physical recoveries. Some people heal better than I, and some stay completely paralyzed. But, two things are certain . . .

Physical healing isn't a given.

Emotional healing is different.

When it comes to grief and loss in life, I know grief will never fully go away. It's too easy to take yourself back to the places in your mind and in your heart where you feel pain and suffering. We'll never be free of burden, but it does get easier.

The thing is I don't think you ever want to move on from grief because, if you do, it's like you've moved on from love. If your loss mattered, why would you ever want to lose those great memories of doing what you love, or spending time with people you love? Remember, there's balance in everything in life, and a life lived without grief would be a life lived without love. Grief is part of the human experience if you live a life full of love.

If I stop hurting when I think about skiing, it would be a tragedy because it would mean I lost the love for it. I don't want to ever leave behind or forget about my loss, but I want to move forward with it.

Think about it—imagine life when you haven't loved and lost. It would be a life deprived of the full human experience—so, I'm going to choose to live passionately with love in my heart even though I know it means I will grieve again—and, when that grief comes, I'll move forward with it, and gratitude will help.

There are things in life we can't change, like a spinal cord injury or the loss of a loved one—but, we have the power to change our perspective. It doesn't matter if it's a loss or an insurmountable obstacle in our way, we can choose optimism. We can choose hope. We can choose to live every day with purpose and presence.

It's our universal right to choose our attitude and effort. It doesn't matter if you wake up in a palace or a prison, everyone has the right to choose attitude and effort. I choose gratitude every day, and it helps. It helps me choose my full effort because, when I experience setbacks, sidesteps, or feeling stuck—which we all do—it helps me see things aren't so bad. It helps frame setbacks, grief, and pain in the grand scheme of things, so I can let it go and move forward.

If your battle is with grief, move forward with it. Don't forget, but forge your new path with gratitude in your heart.

Chapter 21

WHAT'S NEXT?

When the helicopter powered up and the gust of rotor wind hit me? That's when it felt real. With my skis in hand and keeping my head low, I approached the bird from the side, staying within the pilot's sight line. Once inside, headset on, buckled in, I was in for the ride of my life.

It was like an elevator on steroids lifting me hundreds of feet into rarefied air in a matter of seconds and, honestly, the helicopter ride is one of the best parts of heli-skiing. It's something you have to feel to believe—depending on your pilot's daring, it's like riding the ultimate rollercoaster. Only there's no track, and the machine closely follows the contours of the mountain, buzzing past peaks and cliff edges.

From the time I owned my first pair of skis and knew what a helicopter was—at six years old—I wanted to go heli-skiing. It was a goal of mine for a very long time. So, I jumped at the opportunity when I got the chance to get in a helicopter with Ashlin, one of my closest friends and Myles, my long-time mentor and ski coach, as well as pals, Darren and Jan.

We set off from the valley bottom at dawn, just outside Whistler, BC. The sun was rising over the coastal mountain range and, as we gained elevation, cresting over the Pemberton icecap, I could see the skiing terrain come into view.

It was limitless.

The air clear and crisp, there were skiing lines as far as the eye could see.

Our pilot flew along a mountain ridge with a proximity making the hair stand up on the back of my neck, setting down carefully at the top off a mountain peak's ridge line. Blades spinning, he held steady as we disembarked, climbing out one-by-one onto the peak, grabbing our ski gear from the basket. From there, we trudged through deep snow, safely out of range of the rotor blades. Once clear, we gave the pilot the signal, and he took off.

Turbulent chaos consuming the area subsided, and there I was—at the top of the mountain peak. There's a special feeling being in such rugged, remote terrain. It's hard to put into words—no one for miles around. Just me, my friends, and the mountain.

I was back.

I was on top of the world! In a few moments, I was going to live out my vision of skiing wide open powder turns, kicking my spinal cord injury's ass in the process.

Years of work went into getting there. I surfaced from a dark pit, the depths of the deepest valley—a place where I didn't think it was possible to feel any lower. I think it was that perspective making the mountain peak feel so good—my emotional depths gave me the greater emotional capacity to appreciate new highs.

We shared hugs and high fives before gearing up, Jan setting up shots we needed from the ground while Darren filmed from the air. He hung out the side of the helicopter, harnessed in with his camera poised and ready.

The pilot cautioned us to avoid a large crevasse to our right, but the wide open, powder laden glacier off to the left shimmering in the morning sunlight?

Fair game.

"Here goes nothing!" Leading the way, I skied over the ridge, the gentle slope getting steeper and steeper. As I took the turns, I felt the rush again, and I shot my hands up, arms held high above my head, feeling victorious. I was actually skiing again!

Clawing my way back to the top, I put in so much effort, and the path wasn't what I envisioned—but, then again, how much of life goes exactly to plan?

We skied only two runs that day with the helicopter in the air and cameras rolling—which was about all I could handle. My body was exhausted and empty, but my heart was full.

We captured the moment of my dreams.

I still can't feel the skin on my legs or feet to this day, and I struggle with balance and coordination. My strength isn't what it used to be, and my body's internal thermometer and temperature regulation is out of whack. I have tone and spasticity in my muscles, my bowel and bladder still have minds of their own, and my hand dexterity isn't perfect. Metal rods in my neck aren't going anywhere, and I trip and fall. I'm in pain all the time—but, in that instant and every other since, when I feel the forgiving glide of powder beneath my skis, I forget about all I lost, losing myself in the moment.

There's not a day in my life when I'm not reminded I had a spinal cord injury—but, I'm also reminded how lucky I am. It doesn't matter which side of the bed I get out of, I feel gratitude because I can get out of bed. Even if I am, as some would say, 'the luckiest of the unlucky' to have had a spinal cord injury, I don't take my good fortune for granted. I'm grateful every day, and days like the one on the mountain are such a gift.

Life looks very different for me now than it did before I broke my neck. Some relationships I lost, while others survived the test of time—and, some are a result of my trauma.

My career path took a massively different direction, but I'm still choosing to help others, whether it's coaches, athletes, audiences, or companies. I don't coach from the side of a half-pipe anymore—I coach, engage, and inspire people from the stage as well as from my heart. I speak to others as I write this book for you. It's my goal to help you get through the toughest times to overcome challenges and obstacles that were never part of your plan.

I thrive when you thrive.

The bottom line is things happen in life that are never part of the plan. How we react to such situations is what makes the difference between merely surviving or thriving. We think we can plan our lives carefully, and we're set up with what we need to be successful in life. But, what about the curveball?

One of the most, if not the most, important factors in determining whether or not you achieve success in today's ever-evolving world is your ability to overcome adversity. How you handle challenge and stand up in the face of hardship is critical—and, it's true for everyone because no one is immune to difficulties and suffering. In the event you're challenged, how you handle yourself, the mental prep work you undertake, and the self-control with which you approach your problem will dictate your results. You can apply the concepts of mental toughness, resilience, grit, determination, and belief to all aspects of life.

If you face a challenge or trauma that wasn't part of your plan, you have to accept what's happened because there's nothing you can do about it. You can't want what you had, and you have to want whatever you can get in the future. You have to choose the mindset taking you to the next level.

So—if you're working toward a goal, live at your edge. Embrace the uncomfortable. Some people are afraid of what's around the corner, wondering about the consequences of failing. But, what if you fail? It's simple—know you will fail forward. Work relentlessly toward your possibilities. There are a lot of things you can be afraid of in this world, but what's next, isn't one of them.

Remember—life begins at the edge of your comfort zone. That space, when you're pushing the envelope, is where fear, failure, vulnerability, resilience, progress, growth, learning—the magic of life—coexist.

Remind yourself to be grateful, and practice gratitude because when the going gets tough, we can't rely on it in those moments.

When the going gets tough, we need to be ready.

You have it within yourself to push through.

You have it within yourself to thrive.

This story is for you—your obstacles, challenges, and triumphs. I hope it helps you find your next mountaintop because you never know where, when, or how you'll get to your next peak. You just need to start. Take the first step, trusting you have what it takes. If you've been on top before, you can get there again.

When you do get there, make sure you take a moment to enjoy the view.

So, that's it. I challenge you to try overcoming challenges in your way. I know you have it in you. If I can do it, you can do it, too.

That said, I'll leave you with this . . .

What's next for you?

Where's your next mountain peak?

ACKNOWLEDGMENTS

There are so many people to thank for their support, love, and encouragement. I hope you know your friendship and caring carried me through . . .

Thanking my family seems so insignificant—a simple 'thank you' will never be enough for their always having my back. Family first couldn't be more accurate. Dad, Mom, Barry, Anthony, and Gareth—you mean the world to me.

To my dad—thank you for helping shape me into the man I am. You support your people, standing tall for them. A wise soul with a heart of gold . . .

To my grandfather, Anthony T. B. Meyer, who's 96 years of wisdom are in the pages of this book. He learned to walk three times in his life—once naturally, following typhoid fever, and after being blown up by a mortar bomb in WWII—thank you for your wisdom and love. I'll never forget your words, "There will be doldrums, but don't lose heart."

To my amazing mom—you've been there since day one. I wouldn't be who I am without you and, through thick and thin, you always lend me your ear, and you're a pillar to lean on. Your love and compassion—as well as Barry's—lift me up. Your ability to make me feel listened to, loved, and understood is a blessing I don't take for granted.

And, to Jocelyn—you're my rock.

With gratitude,

Mike

PROFESSIONAL ACKNOWLEDGMENTS

CHRYSALIS PUBLISHING AUTHOR SERVICES
L.A. O'NEIL, Editor
www.chrysalis-pub.com
chrysalispub@gmail.com

HIGH MOUNTAIN DESIGN
WYATT ILSLEY, Cover Design
www.highmountaindesign.com
hmdesign89@gmail.com

MIKE SHAW
www.mikeshawski.com
mike@mikeshawski.com

Manufactured by Amazon.ca
Bolton, ON

26175191R00122